MANAGING HUMANS
BITING AND HUMOROUS TALES OF A
SOFTWARE ENGINEERING MANAGER

MANAGING HUMANS

BITING AND HUMOROUS TALES OF A
SOFTWARE ENGINEERING MANAGER

Michael Lopp

Apress®

Managing Humans: Biting and Humorous Tales of a Software Engineering Manager

ISBN-13 (pbk): 978-1-59059-844-3

ISBN-10 (pbk): 1-59059-844-X

Printed and bound in the United States of America 9 8 7 6 5 4 3 2 1

Trademarked names may appear in this book. Rather than use a trademark symbol with every occurrence of a trademarked name, we use the names only in an editorial fashion and to the benefit of the trademark owner, with no intention of infringement of the trademark.

Lead Editor: Jim Sumser
Editorial Board: Steve Anglin, Ewan Buckingham, Gary Cornell, Jason Gilmore, Jonathan Gennick, Jonathan Hassell, James Huddleston, Chris Mills, Matthew Moodie, Jeff Pepper, Dominic Shakeshaft, Jim Sumser, Matt Wade
Project Manager: Beth Christmas
Copy Edit Manager: Nicole Flores
Copy Editor: Damon Larson
Assistant Production Director: Kari Brooks-Copony
Compositor: Darryl Keck
Proofreader: Nancy Riddiough
Indexer: Becky Hornyak
Artist: April Milne
Cover Designer: Kurt Krames
Manufacturing Director: Tom Debolski

Distributed to the book trade worldwide by Springer-Verlag New York, Inc., 233 Spring St., 6th Floor, New York, NY 10013. Phone 1-800-SPRINGER, fax 201-348-4505, e-mail orders-ny@springer-sbm.com, or visit http://www.springeronline.com.

For information on translations, please contact Apress directly at 2855 Telegraph Avenue, Suite 600, Berkeley, CA 94705. Phone 510-549-5930, fax 510-549-5939, e-mail info@apress.com, or visit http://www.apress.com.

To my family.
All of my family.

Contents

ABOUT THE AUTHOR ix

ACKNOWLEDGMENTS xi

PREFACE xiii

PART I
THE MANAGEMENT QUIVER

CHAPTER 1   DON'T BE A PRICK 3

CHAPTER 2   MANAGERS ARE NOT EVIL 7

CHAPTER 3   THE MONDAY FREAKOUT 17

CHAPTER 4   AGENDA DETECTION 21

CHAPTER 5   MANDATE DISSECTION 27

CHAPTER 6   INFORMATION STARVATION 33

CHAPTER 7   SUBTLETY, SUBTERFUGE, AND SILENCE 37

CHAPTER 8   MANAGEMENTESE 43

CHAPTER 9   TECHNICALITY 47

CHAPTER 10   AVOIDING THE FEZ 53

CHAPTER 11   YOUR RESIGNATION CHECKLIST 61

CHAPTER 12   SAYING NO 67

PART II
THE PROCESS IS THE PRODUCT

CHAPTER 13   1.0 73

CHAPTER 14   TAKING TIME TO THINK 83

CHAPTER 15   THE SOAK 89

CHAPTER 16   MALCOLM EVENTS 93

CHAPTER 17   CAPTURING CONTEXT. 99

CHAPTER 18   STATUS REPORTS 2.0 103

CHAPTER 19   TRICKLE THEORY. 107

PART III
VERSIONS OF YOU

CHAPTER 20   A GLIMPSE AND A HOOK 117

CHAPTER 21   NAILING THE PHONE SCREEN 123

CHAPTER 22   NINETY DAYS 127

CHAPTER 23   BELLWETHERS 131

CHAPTER 24   NADD 137

CHAPTER 25   A NERD IN A CAVE 141

CHAPTER 26   MEETING CREATURES 147

CHAPTER 27   INCREMENTALISTS AND COMPLETIONISTS 153

CHAPTER 28   ORGANICS AND MECHANICS 157

CHAPTER 29   INWARDS, OUTWARDS, AND HOLISTICS 163

CHAPTER 30   FREE ELECTRONS 167

CHAPTER 31   RULES FOR THE REORG 171

CHAPTER 32   OFFSHORE RISK FACTOR 177

CHAPTER 33   JOE 181

CHAPTER 34   SECRET TITLES 187

GLOSSARY. 191

INDEX 201

About the Author

Michael Lopp is a veteran engineering manager who has never managed to escape the Silicon Valley. In over 15 years of software development, Michael has worked at a variety of innovative companies including Apple Computer, Netscape Communications, Symantec Corporation, Borland International, and a startup that slowly faded into nothingness.

In addition to his day job, Michael writes a popular technology and management weblog under the nom de plume "Rands," where he discusses his management ideas, worries about staying relevant, and wishes he had time to see more of the world. His weblog can be found at www.randsinrepose.com.

Michael lives in Northern California, never far from the ocean.

Acknowledgments

I'd like to acknowledge and thank Liz Danzico for teaching me about editors and, more importantly, for laughing out loud on the subway while reading early chapters of this book. Both Melle Baker and Jim Sumser took the time to figure out Rands and to remind me who he was when I lost him. The readers of Rands in Repose unwittingly guided the creation of this work by reading, commenting, and mailing. If they hadn't asked for a book, there wouldn't be one.

I wouldn't be a manager without the guidance, insight, and common sense of Tom Paquin.

Preface

This is a work of semi-fiction.

A book on management is filled with insight, ideas, and opinions about how to manage people. All of this information is based on real life experience with actual people who I still know. While I'd love to tell you that all my management experiences have been positive, they haven't. I've lost my shit a couple of times and there were witnesses. These witnesses are the ones who helped me pull it together and gave me another page for this book.

All the names of people referred to in the chapters of this book are fake. I've taken everyone that I've known and mentally thrown them into a bag, shaken said bag, and pulled out Fez, Phil, and Frank. Using these constructed characters, I create a story, sometimes set in a familiar company I actually worked for like Netscape or Borland, which allows me to explain whatever management insight I'm relaying. Like my characters, my stories are fake. My hope is that they still ring true in your head because while they are fantastic stories, they are based on real experiences.

The icing on this semi-fictional cake is Rands. This is a name I began using in the mid-'90s for my virtual presence; when I began weblogging about management, the name stuck. Think of Rands as your semi-fictional guide walking you through the fake stories of fake people that have had incredible relevant (yet fake) experiences.

Rands has a bit of attitude, but, then again, so do I.

THE MANAGEMENT QUIVER

For having shot a bow and arrow maybe ten times in my life, it's odd that I think of management skills as being arrows in a quiver. But the metaphor works. Much of management is about solving problems, and what better way to solve a problem than to tape it to a target, step back, pull out the right arrow, and fire. Whether you hit the target or not, there's a gratifying *plunk* sound. That's the sound of progress.

We all have managers, and whether you're the director of engineering or an individual contributor, one of your jobs is to figure your manager out. What does he want? How does he deal with a crisis? How does he communicate? As you learn each of these lessons, you get an arrow. It's not only a reminder that you learned something, but it's a tool you throw in your quiver so that the next time you see a similar problem, you grab the right arrow, carefully aim, and shoot.

Don't Be a Prick

The beauty of writing for the Web is there really is no plan. I have the luxury to mentally fumble about with any topic. Increasingly, those topics have focused on engineering management, and with the publishing of each article, I receive the occasional "Where's the book?" inquiry. Yeah so, I've always wanted to publish a book, but there's a problem. What's the pitch? *Be a good manager?* Zzzzzzzzz. There are hints of themes among my articles, but there is no single article that sets the stage for the rest; nothing that hints at a basic truth tying my reposing together.

Flash back to the middle of the dot-com implosion. We, the merry crew of the failing startup, are drinking . . . a lot. There are various bars around corporate headquarters, and each has a distinct purpose. There's the dive bar that's great for post-layoff parties. The booze is cheap, and if you're looking to blow off some I'm-really-not-worthless steam, you can pick a fight with the toothless sailor slung over the bar or the guy who just laid you off.

Down the street is the English pub. The beer is better, they have a selection of whiskey, and they have edible food. This is where we get philosophical about the current organizational seizure we're experiencing in our three-year slide toward irrelevancy.

We're there now. We're drinking heavily because the company has just been sold to a no-name public company who will quickly dismantle the one for which we've bled. Everyone knew we'd be here at some point, but no one expected to be the last one standing. And no one expected the CEO to show up.

This isn't the CEO that built the company. He's been gone for over a year. This is the guy the board of directors brought in to sell the startup. Sure, he tried to turn us around, but remember, we're in the middle of a financial nuclear winter here. Money is no longer free.

Those who got a glimpse of the CEO's resume before he arrived knew the gig was up. His last four jobs ended in the company being finely sliced into nothingness. It's called "maximizing shareholder value."

And here we are. Hammered on tequila, the last four from engineering, two guys from tech support . . . and the CEO. Even though we're dizzy with booze, we're fundamentally uncomfortable with the presence of our CEO because we consider him to be an unfeeling prick.

And that's it.

That's the title of my management book.

Don't Be a Prick.

Right, so my editors will probably have an issue with the word "prick" in the title. It falsely implies masculinity to management that is a crock, so we'll call it a working title.

The CEO in question is not a prick. Good guy. Straight talker. Good financial sense. Many failing companies did a lot worse than ours, but that isn't the point. The reason we sat there drunk and uncomfortable was because we had absolutely no connection with this guy. He was the mechanical CEO.

My definition of a great manager is someone with whom you can make a connection no matter where you sit in the organization chart. What exactly I mean by *connection* varies wildly by who you are and what you want and, yes, that means great managers have to work terribly hard to see the subtle differences in each of the people working for them.

See. See the people who work with you. They say repetition improves long-term memory, so let's say it once more. You must see the people who work with you.

If you don't have an inkling of what I'm talking about yet, it might be a good time to set this book down and head over to the programming section of the bookstore because it's time to reconsider that pure engineering career track. Being a manager is a great job (I mean it), but it's your ability to construct an insightful opinion about a person in seconds that will help make you a phenomenal manager. Yes, in a technical management role you need both the left and right sides of the brain, but just because you write great code doesn't mean you're going to have a clue about how to lay off 70 percent of your staff.

Every single person with whom you work has a vastly different set of needs. Fulfilling these needs is one way to make them content and productive. It is your full-time job to listen to these people and mentally document how they are built. This is your most important job. I know the senior VP of engineering is telling you that hitting the date for the project is job number one, but you are not going to write the code, test the product, or document the features. The team is going to do these things, and your job is the team.

Silicon Valley is full of wildly successful dictators. These are the leaders who are successful even though they are world-class pricks. This book is going to push you as far from prickdom as possible, and if that means I'm decreasing the chance you'll end up on the front page of the *Wall Street Journal* labeled a "corporate bulldog with vision," well, I've done my job.

You get to choose the type of manager you will be, and if you want to work with your team—if you want to learn from them, if you want them to trust you—well, I've got some advice for you. Lots of it. Keep reading.

Again, the CEO at the startup was not a prick. He just showed up at the company's wake and assumed that we'd be comfortable with his presence because *he was the CEO*. We knew he was CEO. More importantly, we knew he'd spent exactly zero time using our products. We'd never seen him there on the weekends. Come to think of it, he was never there on Fridays either, because he commuted from another state. We had no shared experience with him other than three strange meaningless all-hands meetings filled with slide projectors, spreadsheets, and monotony.

The CEO believed that these spreadsheet-laden all-hands meetings was all the connection he needed to build a relationship and, for the duration of those meetings, he was right. We felt well-informed after his meetings, but our needs were different a week later when rumors of layoffs started up. They were drastically different a month later when that layoff went down and the CEO was nowhere to be seen.

Organizations of people are constantly shifting around. They are incredibly messy. In this mess, judgments of you and your work will be constructed in moments—in the ten-second conversations you have in the hallway, and in the way you choose to describe who you are.

Meanwhile, you need to constantly assess your colleagues, determine what they need, and figure out what motivates them. You need to remember that what worked one day as a motivational technique will backfire in two months because human beings are confusing, erratic, and emotional. In order to manage human beings in the moment, you've got to be one.

And that's why a better title for this book is: *Managing Humans*.

Managers Are Not Evil

"What, exactly, do you do?"

Slack.

Jawed.

Amazement.

This question is coming from someone I trust. A trusted employee who has been working in my group at the startup for years. This guy always tells me the straight dope and now he's asking me what I do with my day because he honestly does not know.

Let's recap my day. I got to work just after 8 a.m. After my usual 30 minutes of scrubbing and answering e-mail, I did a quick check of tech news, taking a quick pulse of the planet, and then it's off to my first meeting. It's my boss's staff and it runs for almost two hours as usual. After that meeting, I spend 30 minutes digesting notes from that meeting into actual tasks for myself and the team while also tidying the corporate news I received for my staff meeting.

Lunch. I'm eating with the web applications team today. It's 30-plus minutes and then I'm back for bug database scrubbing—a daily 30-minute task before a cross-functional meeting that turned ugly. I needed someone to do something and they are incapable of doing it and that means I'm screwed. After that 60-minute debacle, I've got an hour and a half of one-on-ones. It's during this time that I am asked the lamest question ever: "What, exactly, do you do?"

My first reaction to this question is the wrong one. I want to leap over the table, grab my friend by the shoulders, shake him, and yell, *"While you were uselessly staring at that one bug this morning, I was keeping this organization moving, pal."* My second reaction is to take a deep breath, so I do.

This basic what-do-you-do disconnect between employees and managers is at the heart of why folks don't trust their managers or find them to be evil.

There Is Evil

My background: I've worked at six different companies in the past 15 years. In those years, I've had ten different jobs ranging from QA engineer to director of engineering. Similarly, I've worked for a variety of managers, from first-line managers to CEOs. I've never worked outside of engineering, but, especially in the senior management roles, I've been exposed to the inner workings of the vastly different functional groups that make up a company.

I've seen a lot of varieties of organizational pride and panic. At both Borland and Netscape, I experienced the company vibe as it shifted from "We're the Microsoft killer!" to "We're screwed!" At the startup, I showed up as employee number 20 and it watched it grow to 250 employees before the Internet bubble eroded the company to 50 folks wondering what to do with all the extra hardware.

These drastic shifts in organization perceptions showed me managers who were great at the pride part, but turned into jerks when the panic started. Likewise, new leaders and lessons showed up during the panic—leaders who were quietly getting their work done during the pride.

In all of this, I can count the number of truly evil people I worked with on one hand. There are evil managers out there. I apologize, I lied in the title of this chapter. These are genuinely evil and mean people. There are fewer than you think, but they are out there and my only advice is, upon detection, to run away as quickly as possible.

Your Manager's Job

The first and most basic frustration folks have with the management is the easiest to explain. You are frustrated because you're busting your ass, but each time you walk by your boss's offices he's got his feet kicked up on the table, coffee in one hand, the other hand jumping hither 'n' fro, and he's talking to some guy you don't know. How in the world could this be work?

Here's the deal: your manager's job is not your job.

Ever had a meeting with a completely different part of your company? Maybe it's engineering and facilities and you're talking about getting additional space for your team. Your goal is clear, "I need more space," but once the meeting kicks off, you realize that you and facilities are speaking a different language. It's English, but the context is wildly different. Those facilities guys are rambling about lease agreements, safety codes, and scads of unfamiliar acronyms. In five minutes, it's clear that you have no idea what they really do.

Before that meeting, if I asked you what the role of facilities was in your company, you would've scrunched your face and mumbled something about cube construction. I trust that, like me, you're an optimist and you believe that everyone in your company is busily working on whatever they do. I also believe the fact that you don't understand what they do automatically biases you. You believe that because you understand your job intimately, it is more important than anyone else's.

In your head, you are king. It's clear what you do; it's clear what is expected of you. There is no person who rules you better than yourself because you know exactly what you're about. Anyone outside of your head is a mystery because they are not you. In a social situation, it's entertaining to figure out what another person is about, but in an employee/manager situation, there's more at stake. Who is this guy who decides whether or not I get a raise? What's he saying to my VP about me? Does he see me as a success or a failure? Who is that guy in his office anyway? *What does he do all day?*

I am not going to explain what your manager does all day. Sorry.

I am going to hand you six critical questions that you need to answer in order to figure out if this guy is capable of looking out for number one—you. Ideally, you'd be able to get answers to these questions before you took a new job, but you didn't and now you're working for a manager who isn't speaking your language. These questions might give you insight into where he's coming from.

Where Does Your Manager Come From?

I'm going to start and finish here because the pedigree of your manager determines not only how you should communicate, but also what to expect when the shit hits the fan.

Ironically, the second most common complaint I've heard from frustrated employees is, "My manager has no idea what I do." It's good to know the problem goes both ways, no? There are a couple of possible causes for this situation. Your manager may not care what you are doing. It doesn't mean the work you are doing is good or bad, it's just not on his radar. Some folks find this arrangement of ignorance to be a cozy, warm blanket. It's a no-fuss job. No awkward hallway conversation, just me and my code and . . . I'm what? I'm fired? Holy shit. Well, that's the risk of having a covert job. No one knows your value, which puts you first in line when it's time to trim the workforce.

Another likely situation is that your manager doesn't actually understand what you're doing because he was never an engineer. I'm not talking about the prequalified disasters where some brainiac on senior staff decided it was a good idea to put the head of marketing in charge of engineering, I'm talking about the engineering managers who are hiding the fact they never really did much coding. Sure, they can talk the talk and they're buzzword-compliant, but what was their last programming assignment? What piece of code are they really proud of? Is their degree in computer science?

If you're getting vague answers full of words that sound right, my guess is you've got a faker on your hands. I'm talking about someone who has managed to wedge their way into a position of engineering leadership on their chutzpah and not their technical ability. You're not automatically screwed in this scenario. A person who can convince the organization they've got leadership ability and hide the fact they haven't a clue what a pointer is . . . has, well, moxie.

This person has spent their entire career wondering, "When are they going to figure me out?" This paranoia has given them solid information-detection skills, which can be useful to you and your organization. They know when the layoff is coming, they know how to talk to senior management, but they don't know how to talk to you because you're actively, passionately doing something they're clueless about and they believe they have to maintain the appearance they know what they're doing.

If this is your manager and you believe there is value in what they do, your job is to figure out how to speak their language. Maybe they snuck out of QA? OK, then speak QA. Maybe they just never got around to that computer science degree? OK, take the time to teach them about your work. I'm not talking teaching this guy C++, I'm talking 15 minutes at the whiteboard with flowcharts. This is *what I do* and this is *why it matters*.

Your manager is your face to the rest of the organization. Right this second, someone you don't know is saying something great about you because you took five minutes to pitch your boss on your work. Your manager did that. You gave him something to say.

How Are They Compensating for Their Blind Spots?

Now we're going to pick on your favorite manager. Tell me about him. Probably a great communicator, funny guy; charismatic, you say? He probably inspired you. You can probably quote a few of his more infamous sayings. "Better is the enemy of done." The question is, what were his blind spots?

Each manager, good or bad, is going to have a glaring deficiency. Maybe he did escape from QA and now he's the director of engineering. Perhaps he's a stunning technologist with absolutely no sense of humor. The question is, does he recognize he has a blind spot?

I ask the same question in every interview I have: "Where do you need help?" Whether it's an individual contributor, a manager, or my new boss, I'm always curious where a person sees their weaknesses. A flippant "I'm solid across the board" response is a terrifying red flag. I'm a fan of pride; I want you to sell yourself in a interview, but if you suggest that you're flawless, all I'm thinking is that your flaws are so big that you can't talk about them or you have no clue what they are.

A manager's job is to take what skills they have, the ones that got them promoted, and figure out how to make them scale. They do this by building a team that accentuates their strengths and, more importantly, reinforces where they are weak. Dry technologists need team members who are phenomenal communicators, folks who can tell a joke and socially glue the organization together. Those vision guys with zero technology chops need you, the strong technologist, to tell them what is technically possible.

A manager's job is to transform their glaring deficiency into a strength by finding the best person to fill it and trusting him to do the job.

Does Your Manager Speak the Language?

OK, so you're in a square room. There are two clear windows in this room, one on each side. In front of each window is a microphone which, when turned on, pipes whatever you say to whomever is on the other side of the window. Now, your manager is on the other side of one window and your best work friend is behind the other. It's Friday, and I want you to give your weekly status report to your friend. Something like: "Monday was a disaster. I got in late because I whooped it up on Sunday night. Took a stab at the spec, but left a little early because I was hungover. Tuesday and Wednesday were pretty good. Finished the spec, closed some bugs, went to the cross-functional review, got some good feedback. You should read the current version. Thursday was meeting hell. Got nothing done. Three useless hours. Friday, well, I had a beer at lunch and I'm leaving early."

Now, spin around and give your status to your boss.

I do not care if you work for the world's best manager. I do not care if he was the best man in your wedding. You are going to give a vastly different sequence of events because you are not talking to a person when you talk with your manager; you are talking to the organization. You instinctively know that telling your boss that you had a beer at lunch is a bad idea, not because he'd know it, but because the organization would.

The language you are speaking when you talk to your manager is a flavor of managementese (see Chapter 8 for more on managementese). Yeah, the language that Scott Adams has made millions of dollars exploiting. It is a carefully constructed language that is designed to convey information across the organization. Managementese allows managers from very different parts of the organization to communicate even though their respective jobs are chock-full of different acronyms and proper names. And yeah, managementese sounds funny.

An example: "Our key objective for this project is the schedule. We need to keep our teams focused on their respective goals, but also keep them cross-pollinating so they can error correct on their own."

When you hear that, you think, "Why can't he talk like a human?" He's not talking to you. He's talking to other managers and he's saying some very Rands-like things, like "Commitments matter!" and "The team is smarter than the individual!" It'd be great if managers could speak with a little more art, but the job at hand is to spread information across the organization as efficiently as possible. And a local dialect of managementese is the best way.

Besides, they still need to talk to you, which leads us to . . .

How Does Your Manager Talk to You?

My first piece of advice to all new managers is "Schedule one-on-ones, keep them on the same day and time, and never cancel them." With this mind, some of the trickiest transitions for me during the day are when these one-on-ones show up. I'm deep in some problem, writing a specification, answering a critical e-mail, and this person walks in my office and they want to talk about I don't know what . . . *I'm working in the zone here, people.* In the brief second I try to figure out some way to reschedule this meeting, I remind myself of a simple rule, "You will always learn something in your one-on-one."

When is your manager giving you a chance to tell him what's in your brain? I'm worried if your answer isn't "at a one-on-one," but I'm not panicking, yet. Maybe your manager is one of these organic types who likes to jump you in the hallway and gather relevant bits. Terrific. Does he do it consistently or when he needs something? The former is great; the latter is a problem waiting to happen.

What is a manager learning in a one-on-one? Much of what you're talking about in a one-on-one your manager already knows. You're concerned about the reorg, right? Well, everyone is and he's already talked to four other people about their concerns. You think the field engineers are a bunch of twits? So does he. A good manager has his finger on the pulse of their organization and the one-on-one usually echoes much of that pulse, so why is he carving out 30 minutes for every person on his team?

He wants to learn.

Whether it's a one-on-one or a random hallway conversation, your manager should always be in active information acquisition. He should love it when you stop him in the hallway and tell him, "I hate your favorite feature." See, the thing was, he's been losing sleep over that feature for the past three days and he can't figure out why. Your random hatred just shoved his thinking in another direction.

Managers who don't have a plan to regularly talk to everyone on their team are deluded. They believe they are going to learn what is going on in their group through some magical organizational osmosis and they won't. Ideas will not be discovered, talent will be ignored, and the team will slowly begin to believe what they think does not matter, and the team is the company.

How Much Action per Decision?

When the new VP showed up for his first day at the startup, he was wearing a Members Only jacket. Sky blue. I didn't know they still made these throwbacks to the '80s. A jacket that lived under the tagline, "When you put it on, something happens." I'd given the VP a thumbs up during the button-up and tie phase of the interview, so I gave him the benefit of the doubt.

Three months in, we had a problem. Members Only was doing a phenomenal job of discussing and dissecting the problems facing engineering. We'd leave meetings fresh with new ideas and promises of improvements, but then nothing would happen. OK, so follow-up meeting. WOW! He gets it. I'm fired up again. Let's roll. Ummm, two more weeks and nothing is happening here.

Now, me being the director of engineering, you can argue that the onus of action was on me. Problem was, I was doing everything I signed up to do. The VP wasn't. He wasn't talking with the CEO about our new plans. He wasn't handling the other director who was totally checked out. When the third follow-up meeting was scheduled, the VP again demonstrated his solid problem-solving skills, but I wasn't listening anymore. I was waiting for when we got the next-steps portion of the conversation where I'd pull up the meeting notes from the previous two meetings and carefully point out these were the same next steps as *the last two meetings*.

The act of delegation is a slippery slope for managers. Yes, you want to figure out how not to be a bottleneck in your organization and, yes, you want to figure out how to scale, but you also want to continue to get your hands dirty. Members Only's problem was he believed his job was purely strategic. Think big thoughts; delegate the results of those thoughts to the minions. He was a pure delegator and he'd forgotten how to do real work.

Pure delegators are slowly becoming irrelevant to their organizations. The folks who work for pure delegators don't rely on them for their work because they know they can't depend on them for action. This slowly pushes your manager out of the loop and, consequently, his information about what is going on in his organization becomes stale. Then, the CEO walks into your boss's office and asks, "How's it going?" The third time your boss gives the same generic answer, the CEO goes to you and asks the same question. When you respond with, "Well, we're fucked," the CEO has an entire other conversation with your manager.

Real work is visible action managers take to support their particular vision for their organization. The question you need to answer for your manager is simple: does he do what he says he's going to do? Does he make something happen?

The New Guy

Back at Netscape, Internet Explorer was threatening, but we were under the illusion the sky was not falling. We were merrily planning the next release of the browser under the assumption that Microsoft was going to somehow screw up their browser. Besides, it wasn't about the browser anymore; it was about owning the entire desktop. Yes, someone was actually suggesting the browser wasn't an application; it was an *operating system, people*. The perception of unlimited money makes people stunningly stupid, by the way. Anyhow, of course, everyone at Netscape wanted to be on the "next-generation browser" project. We were just waiting for the execs to crown a director to run the effort.

When the promotion came and it was some engineering manager from an acquired company we'd never heard of, heads were scratched. Until that time, the core engineering team at Netscape was a private club. We'd expected one of our long-time proven managers to the lead the effort. Nope, Mike the New Guy got it and, in a week, he went from no name to the hottest ticket on Middlefield Road.

What happened? Well, turns out the engineering managers were playing a lot of roller hockey and, while they played, Mike the New Guy was working it. He was chatting it up with the execs, getting to know the relevant *players*, *pawns*, and *free electrons* in the organization (see Chapter 4 for more about players and pawns, and Chapter 30 for more on free electrons). Mike the New Guy was hungry. He was driven, and after six months of incessantly demonstrating this hunger, the execs gave him the keys to the executive washroom. Mike the New Guy was a made guy.

Just like delegation, the act of navigating politics in an organization is slippery. The difference between a manager who knows what's going on in an organization and one who is a purely politically driven slimeball is thin. I would take either of those over some passive manager who lets the organization happen to him. Politically active managers are informed managers. They know when change is afoot and they know what action to take to best represent their organization in that change.

Of all the questions in this chapter, understanding your manager's place in the political food chain is the trickiest because you're often not in the meetings where he is interacting with his superiors. Those are the situations where you understand what their view is of him and, therefore, his organization. The next best gauge of your manger's political clout is cross-functional meetings where his peers are present. How are they treating him? Is it a familiar conversation or are they getting to know him? Should they know him? If it's his meeting, is he driving it? If it's not his meeting, can he actively contribute?

The organization's view of your manager is their view of you. I'm glad you're a C++ rock star, but the problem is, your manager is a passive non-communicator who doesn't take the time to grok the political intrigue that is created by any large group of people. I see him as a non-factor and you're living in the shadow of a non-factor.

Sorry.

What Happens When They Lose Their Shit?

Pride and panic. The two delicious ends of the management spectrum. Pride is when it's going swimmingly. Great product release, selling well. Hired that phenomenal guy from the other group who is going to totally write us another fabulous product. More requisitions in the pipeline. Golly, I can't imagine it going better, can you?

Getting to pride is usually the end result of a lot of work and a little luck. What you can learn from your manager in this phase is how they'll deal with that swelling head of theirs. Do they take care of those who got them there? Do they have a plan for what's next? All of these are interesting developments, but they don't show you half as much as panic and there is no bigger panic than a layoff.

Your manager is not a manager until they've participated in a layoff. I mean it. I know he fired that one Fez and he hired a bunch of the team, but those are individual, isolated activities (see Chapter 10 for more about the Fez). He hasn't truly represented the company until he actively participates in the constructive deconstruction of an organization. There is no more pure a panic than a layoff, and you want to see who your manager will become because it's often the first time he sees the organization is bigger than the people.

A layoff is a multi-month affair. By the time it's been announced on the front page of CNET, it's been bouncing around the boardroom and your boss's staff meeting for a couple of weeks. This means your boss has been staring at you for the past couple of weeks in one-on-ones and ignoring everything you say because he's trying to figure out how to lay off half of his staff. You are very interested in who he becomes during this time because that is actually the person you've been working for these past few years.

Once you've got a confirmed layoff, you need to go back to each of the questions on this list and ask them again. How is he talking to you? How is talking with the organization? What is he doing to make up for the fact that pretty much everything stops in a company when a layoff is leaked? Is he staying politically active? Or is he checking out? All of these observations teach you about your boss and, conveniently, give you insight into whether or not you should be looking for another gig.

Panic backs a person into a corner and their only means of getting out of that corner is relying on skills that have worked for them in the past. This is how a normally friendly manager can turn into a backstabbing asshole when it comes to a layoff. See, they were an asshole before; you just weren't there to see it. If you are lucky enough to see this behavior as well as make it through the layoff, well, you learned two things. First, this guy I work for degrades to jerk when the sky falls. Second, he values me enough to keep me around. The question remains: are you going to hang around waiting for him to be a jerk to you?

The Big Finish

When the first layoff hit Borland, I was two years into my QA stint. I don't remember wondering what a layoff was and I don't remember wondering if I was going to lose my job. What I remember is the senior VP of applications, who walked around the building, gathered the product team up, and then told us the straight dope about the layoff . . . in the hallway. This is what the layoff is about, this is who is affected, and this is when it's happening. I'd never interacted with Rob in my life and, come to think of it, I never really interacted with him again. Still, I think fondly of the guy because during a time of stress, he illuminated, he didn't obfuscate.

A successful organization is built of layers of people that are glued together with managers. Each layer is responsible for a broad task, be it engineering or QA or marketing. Between each layer is a manager whose job it is to translate from one layer to the next . . . in both directions. He knows what his employees want. He knows what his manager wants, and he's able to successfully navigate when those wants differ.

The way he navigates these waters is by knowing the answer to two questions. Question #1: Where did I come from? Being able to relate to those you manage comes from intimately understanding their job. It allows you to speak their language. Question #2: Where am I going? A plan for your manager's next big move is his incentive. It puts him in the uncomfortable position of trying to discern the murky political motivations of the major influencers of your company. It might not be a skill set he has, but he's never going to stop trying because he knows where he wants to go. He's got a map defined by his motivation.

Why do you care that your boss wants to be VP of software? You care because his success is your success. If he doesn't know that, he might be evil.

The Monday Freakout

Mondays start on Sunday. It's the moment you realize that the weekend is over and you begin staring at the endless list of things to do that you began to ignore early Friday as the sweet, sweet smell of the weekend filled your office.

As a rule, the earlier on Sunday that you think about Monday is an indication of how much you neglected to do on Friday. Worse, the more time you spend during your weekend fretting about your weekdays, the more pissed off you're going to be when Monday actually arrives. The extreme case is when someone spends the entire weekend working themselves into a frustrated knot of stress regarding their work situation, and that means, when Monday arrives, they might freak out.

This Monday's freakout was courtesy of my QA lead, Dingfelder. He was simmering in the hallway all morning. He was talking in sharp, hushed tones to anyone who would listen. I already knew about the topic, but I was surprised by his verbal intensity. Right after lunch, he struck. Hands tightly folded in front of him, Dingfelder stood in my door, lightly bouncing on the front of his feet. He was about to . . .

"Rands, can we talk for a minute?"

Shit.

We walked into the nearest conference room; I gripped the table and braced myself.

"Dear lord, we're going to ship horrible product and you're setting unrealistic deadlines and QA always gets the shaft and do we support Internet Explorer 7 and my credibility is on the line here and Jesus Christ didn't we learn our last time please I hate HTML and this developer keeps on diddling with shit."

Rands Rule of Software Management #27: If someone is going to freak out, it's going to be on a Monday.

Freakouts are unique because of their intensity. The first time you're on the receiving end, you'll be unable to catch your breath because of the shock. How did this usually calm person end up yelling in my face? Let's not worry about that right now. Let's first understand how to deal with the freakout in front of you, and that means following the rules.

Don't Participate in the Freakout

The worst type of freakout is one that is purely emotional, illogical, and based on little to no fact. It also lacks any type of solution because there really isn't a well-defined problem except that this person really needs to freak out. The volume and intensity of this type of freakout can be negatively intoxicating and you'll be tempted to jump on the freakout bandwagon.

Don't.

The best move here is to simply listen and maintain eye contact. Your calmness is a primal attempt to telepathically reflect the insanity back to the freak so they'll realize they've gone off the deep end. This can be rough because the freakout may be pointed directly at you, but even under attack, your job is the same. Listen. Nod. Repeat.

Give the Freak the Benefit of the Doubt

Chances are, your freak really does have something to say, but maybe they've lost perspective spending every waking moment stressing since last Friday at 5 p.m. Perhaps their freakout has nothing to do with what they're saying and has everything to do with an unrelated series of events the previous week that ended poorly and has mutated into this freakout. Maybe they drink too much coffee, but remember, they have a point.

In any freakout, there is normally a very noisy preamble which is designed to get your attention. Dingfelder's comments above are all preamble. I know after he stops to take a breath that we're going to get to the heart of the matter. He's probably already said it, but when he says it again, "Unrealistic deadlines," I know we have progress because we've hit on the foundation of the freakout and we can begin a conversation which is the first step to defusing this situation.

But, it's not always that easy . . .

Hammer the Freak with Questions

Sometimes the preamble just doesn't end. Sure, there's content in there somewhere, but some freaks really just like the freak. They like that they have your attention, or maybe they just like to hear their voice, but if it's been a couple of minutes and all you're hearing is preamble, it's time to grab the reins.

Ending the preamble and starting the conversation starts with a question. Why is the product going to be horrible? Should we care about IE 7? Properly timed and well-constructed questions lead your freak away from emotion because they force them to the other side of their brain where they don't freak, they think.

I was lucky; I knew Dingfelder was about to drop the bomb a good two hours before he got around to it. In that time, I leapt into our bug tracking system to figure out how many bugs each person had filed; I glanced at bug severities, arrival rates, and any other juicy bug tidbits that might help me defuse the bomb.

Once the Dingfelder freakout began, I calmly pulled my bug notes out. The moment he took his breath, I asked, "Hey, so how many bugs showed up this weekend? How many did we fix? How many of those fixes didn't take? Wow, why do you think that happened?"

The key with a question offense is to move your freak from the emotional state to the rational one. I know I know and I know how good it feels when you're stressed out to attack the source of that stress in what looks like a rational manner, but, um, you're yelling, pointing your finger at me, and jumping up and down. Do you want me to react to the yelling or to the facts?

Get the Freaks to Solve Their Own Problems

One pleasant side effect of attacking freakouts with questions is that you discover the freak is often already close to a solution. Remember, they've been simmering since Friday and, in that time, they've been chewing on the problem from every angle possible. In that time, their understanding, while soaked in emotion, has more depth than yours.

Even if you haven't successfully predicted a freakout, you can still use your experience as a means of exploring the freak's understanding of whatever the issue might be. Heck, you don't even need experience; all you need is the desire to understand what this person is freaking out about. Sometimes, you get lucky. Your simple clarification questions end up with an "And *dammit Rands*, the engineering managers should be *scrubbing their bugs every morning!*"

OK.

Let's do that.

You Still Have a Problem

Being emotionally invested in what you are doing is an absolute requirement for caring about your job. What I hear when you walk into my office and freak out is "I'm caring about my job here, Rands, please listen." It's taken years of weathering these explosions to hear this and not to take it personally, but I've come to expect that freakouts are a normal event in passionate engineering teams.

It's still a management failure.

It's great that your freak has chosen to freak out. The alternative is that they're not saying a thing and have decided to leave the company. The fact that your particular Dingfelder is screaming at you in your office is a good sign that he's not leaving because he clearly, loudly cares.

But you screwed up. Someone is screaming in your office, and once you successfully defuse the situation, you know two things. First, there is a problem that needs to be solved. Second, and more importantly, someone believes the best way to get your attention is by freaking out.

Agenda Detection

I hate meetings.

Everyone hates them because we've all been to so many that have sucked unequivocally that we now walk into a conference room, sit down with our arms folded, and think, "OK, how long until this one is officially a waste of my time? How long until *this* one sucks?" And then it does. Time is wasted. Hot air is generated and everyone sits around the table wondering when someone is going to stop the madness.

If you've ever been frustrated in a meeting—if you've sat there wondering why in the world these people, these managers, who are paid the big bucks to move the company along, simply can't do or say the painfully obvious—then keep reading.

There is a basic skill you need whenever you walk into a meeting that has suck potential. This skill is important whether you're a participant or the person running the meeting. The skill is called *agenda detection*.

Simply put, agenda detection is the ability to discern

1. Typical meeting roles and how meeting participants assume them

2. Explanation of what these distinct meeting roles want out of a meeting

3. How to use this understanding to get the hell out of the meeting as quickly as possible

The first step in getting out of a meeting is to identify what kind of meeting it is. A meeting agenda would help, but as most meetings proceed without one, you're on your own. Chances are you're either in an informational meeting or a conflict resolution meeting.

At informational meetings—big surprise coming here, folks—information is passed on. Think your favorite quarterly all-hands meeting. Staff meetings. Any meeting where there's a standing assumed agenda. There are two kinds of participants in these meetings: talkers and listeners.

Roles and agendas in these meetings are simple. Talkers are talking and listeners are listening. Get it? There is no problem to be solved other than the transmission of information. The quicker it happens, the sooner everyone is back to work.

You can quickly identify those folks who don't get this. They're the whack jobs who always ask the same (or random) questions during an all-hands with the hope that simply by asking, they're going to change something. It's a noble act, speaking your mind in front of all your peers. But it's also a waste of time. This is an informational meeting, people. The talkers are here to pass on whatever organizational knowledge they need to so as to prevent a rebellion. Folks are here to nod, not solve problems. When the whack job speaks up, everyone who understands the nature of the meeting is thinking, "OK, another useless question that's going to keep me here longer. Crap."

At a conflict resolution meeting, some problem needs to be solved. Apparently, it could not be resolved via e-mail, instant messaging, or hallway conversations, so some bright fellow decided to convene a face-to-face meeting where the bandwidth is high and the time wastage is significant.

Agenda detection in the conflict resolution meeting is more complex. To see it in action, let's create a meeting:

Tuesday, 4 p.m. List of suspects: You: Joe Senior Engineer, two other random engineers, one product management person, and a program manager. The program manager called the meeting to solve a problem your team had nothing to do with, so you're already resentful of being here in the first place. See, the sales folks sold something that your company does not make. You're here to explain how much it would cost to build this thing that you've never built before but that's already been sold. Been here? Thought so.

Agenda detection starts by first classifying the players. There are two major types that you need to identify: *players* and *pawns*. The simple distinction between the two types is that players want something out of the meeting. This is their incentive to participate. They'll be leaning forward, actively nodding, barely able to hold themselves back from spilling their agenda all over the table.

Pawns are either silent or instruments of running the meeting. In either case, they're adding very little to the meeting and can be removed from strategic consideration. The term *pawns* is not intended to be derogatory, of course. Pawns very well might be running your company, but in meetings, they don't contribute . . . it's just not their key skill.

The bucketing of players and pawns is simple. You can do it with the attendee list and a bit of organizational knowledge. Let's try it with our hypothetical meeting mentioned previously.

First, you can assume all the engineers are players. They obviously have technical knowledge they may throw on the table, otherwise why were they invited? The product management person is also a player as she represents the sales folks in this meeting. Program managers in these meetings are pawns. They'll make sure action items are recorded and that the meeting ends on time.

Meeting Bail Tip #1: Identify the Players

If you're sitting in a meeting where you're unable to identify any players, get the hell out. This is a waste of your time. These are meetings traditionally called by windbags who like to hear themselves talk, but hold no real influence over the organization/product/whatever. Unfortunately, if you're new to a group, you need to get burned by the windbags a few times before you learn to avoid these totally fucking useless meetings. It's tough being the new guy.

The next step in agenda detection now kicks in as we look at the players. This is when you figure out each player's position relative to the issue on the table. For whatever that issue is there are two subclasses of players: the *pros* and the *cons*.

The pros are the players who are currently on the winning side of the issue. They're getting what they want and are not incented to negotiate. They don't even have to be here, and yet, they're here and appear willing to listen to the cons, right? Maybe. Maybe they're just here to watch the cons squirm.

The cons, clearly, are the ones who are being screwed. They're likely the ones who yelled loudly enough to get the meeting set up in the first place. Cons are usually easy to pick out because they're expressing some degree of pissed-off-ed-ness.

Meeting Bail Tip #2: Identify the Pros and Cons

Like our player requirement, both pros and cons must be represented for any progress to occur, otherwise you're just going to talk and talk and talk. You're guaranteed the cons are going to be present because they're the ones scream-ing and shouting. If you want the meeting to produce something useful, the pros must be represented. The specific pro does not need to be in the build-ing, but they must have a designated proxy, or the cons will bitch, heads will nod, and *nothing* will happen.

Let's take a stab at identifying the pros and cons in our hypothetical meeting.

In the previous example, it's clearly engineering who are being asked to build a product *that does not exist*. They're pissed and they've called this meeting to quantify this frustration. Hello, cons.

As we've already identified our program manager as a pawn, we can only assume that our product manager is the pro. But wait, now you're in this meeting and she sounds like an engineer. "Those goddamned sales folks. What the hell were they thinking? This is the last time, blah, blah, blah . . ." She trails off into everyone's frustrations, and you're back to square one trying to figure out who's who in this mess.

Our product manager suddenly appears to be a con. Does this mean Rands thinks I should pull the ripcord and get the hell out? No, your product manager's the pro, all right; she's just bright enough not to let anyone know it. A common tactic of a good pro is to not acknowledge that they're the pro. This means that they don't actually have to take the heat for whatever the conflict is. The real pros, in this example, the sales folks who cut our brilliant impossible deal, aren't in the room, they're out in the field, cutting *more* unachievable deals. The product manager is attempting to fake out the engineers in the room by saying, "Hey, this is a tough problem that *they* have put *us* in. What are *we* going to do?" Brilliant bait-and-switch, no? Don't sweat it. They make less than you.

The stage is set. Our pawns have been filtered out; our sneaky pro is nodding, placating with her feigned commiseration; the cons are yelling; and yes, you're still in the meeting.

Believe it or not, the hard part is done.

If you've paid attention, you've got a pretty good map of who's who, and where the whos are, so now all you need to do is figure out what the whos want. The pawns don't want anything; they were just happy to be invited. The pros are there to show off their complete and utter ownership of the issue. They'll leave whenever, the sooner the better.

So the reason you're sitting there is the cons. What do they want? I'm convinced that the majority of meetings on this planet go long and do little because the people sitting around the table simply do not figure out who the hell they're talking to and what they want.

Stop. You've got a meeting in mind, some horrible meeting where the issue is so complex that there's no way the simple identification process I described could apply. Wrong. You're jumping to solve the issue and that's where everyone fucks this up. Who cares about the issue? Do you know who matters in whatever horrible meeting you're sitting in? Did you take the time to identify the people who actually care—the ones who can make a difference? If you didn't, you deserve every useless minute of that meeting.

So yes, the cons *do* want something here. You're going to meet their needs in order to get out the door and their needs are simple—so simple you're going to laugh. The cons need a plan, some assurance that will somehow address whatever the issue is. Doesn't matter if that plan comes from the pawn, the player, the pro, the con . . . Someone needs to synthesize everything into constructive next steps and *communicate that to* the cons, and then you're done. You're out the door.

Doesn't need to be a great plan, or an honest plan, or even a complete plan. Cons will not let you out of that meeting until there is the perception of forward progress. If you've scheduled an hour and that hour is up, you're thinking, "Well, that's one way out." Again, incorrect, because the cons are returning to their desks and scheduling a follow-up meeting where the organizational ineptitude is going to continue.

Meeting Bail Tip #3: Figure Out the Issue

You might very well have the requisite players, pros, and cons, but then again, you might have too many. If it's 30 minutes in and you still can't figure out what the issue is, it's time to go: too many issues. Someone who cares more than you needs to distill this chaos down to a coherent statement so the pros and cons can argue about one thing.

Meetings are always going to be inefficient because language is hard. Getting folks in the same group, with the same organizational accent, to talk coherently to each other is hard enough. Meetings give us the opportunity to include other organizations with other accents. This makes the language chaos complete. Now, you don't care. You don't need to know what they're saying because with agenda detection, you can figure out who they are, what they want, get it for them, and get the hell out.

Mandate Dissection

In your quiver of management skills, you've got a couple of powerful arrows. There's the annual review where you take the time to really explain, in detail, what a given employee needs to do to grow. That's huge. That can be life changing. That's a big arrow. How about the layoff? That's when you get asked who stays and who goes. You're going to lose some sleep when you've got to pull the bow back on that one.

Then there's the mandate. The mandate is when you gather the team together and calmly say, "This is the way it is." No Q&A. No collaboration. It's your dictate handed down from on high.

Most folks have learned to despise the mandate.

Rewind a few years back. I'm at my prior gig and we've just hired a new VP who I really liked. This guy was sharp, experienced, had a litany of name brand companies on his resume, and he could tell a joke. Sold. Hired.

He was pretty quiet the first few weeks, checking out the landscape, sitting in on various meetings and listening. Engineering was in the process of discussing some drastic new directions for our products, and the incrementalists (ship it soon!) were doing battle with the completionists (ship it when it's done!). Tensions were high. Finger pointing, yelling . . . all the things you aren't supposed to do in business, but *they feel so good* when you *know you're right*.

The VP's second month arrived and we were still yelling. In my Wednesday one-on-one with the VP, he simply told me, "We are going to do it like this. End of discussion."

Right, so of course I started spewing, "See, we still had to resolve issue #27 and, boy, were the completionists going to be pissed and had you thought about risk #12A?" He let me go for a while and then he repeated himself, "We are going to do it like this. End of discussion."

I might have nodded, I don't remember.

As predicted, the team freaked. One completionist assured us he was going to quit. He slammed his door. The incrementalists weren't happy either because they didn't like being told what to do. They like to run the show. We had a good solid week of organizational disarray and then we got back to work.

The new VP employed the mandate. He said, "I'm the guy who's telling you the way it is."

Now remember, I liked this guy, but in the back of my mind when someone gives me an order, I don't hear the order, I hear "Shut up, get moving, I don't care what you think." Your job as a manager is to avoid giving this impression at all costs because it eventually erodes your credibility. I'll tell you how.

There are three distinct phases to the mandate: Decide, Deliver, and Deliver (Again). Since you are the ultimate decision maker regarding this particular matter, we're going to call this a *local mandate*. These are opposite of *foreign mandates*, which we'll talk about later. Let's begin.

Decide

Your first step is to decide when to employ the mandate and to also understand what the consequences are. There are thousands of little tiny decisions you and your team make during the course of a day. A majority of these decisions come and go and no one is the wiser. Every so often, a big decision comes along. Doesn't matter what the content is, what matters is that some portion of your team is on one side of the decision and another group is on the other side and they're arguing.

Collaboration, cross-pollination, debating, arguing. Whatever you want to call the process, well, it doesn't always work. Sometimes the team is so polarized that they start confusing the emotion with the decision. Rather than arguing the facts, they begin to argue from their heart and that is when you need to consider the mandate. Rule of thumb: When the debate is no longer productive, it's time to make a decision.

My management style is to allow the team to argue as long as possible. I've got a collaborative management style because I know that the more brains and more time the team spends staring at an idea, the stronger the idea becomes. This means that decision-making in groups that I manage tends to be slower because I'm busy cross-pollinating. Consequently, I'm certain it means our output is higher quality because we've taken the time to consider what the hell we're doing.

Remember that for every person on the team who has a strong opinion regarding the decision, there are probably four other coworkers who just want someone to make a decision so that they can get back to work. We've each been part of the silent majority before. It's the time when you choose to not engage in the heated debate. Maybe because you're doing actual work or perhaps you just don't care. You appreciate your silent status as you see the debate rage in the hallway and realize how much pain, sweat, and tears you saved by staying out of it. When the team is still yapping away two weeks later, you start to wonder when someone is going to shut these people up.

Mandates are the friend of the silent majority. Even if you really annoy the concerned parties, the silent majority will appreciate the peace and quiet once you've delivered your verdict.

Deliver

The purpose of this article is not to explain how to make whatever hard decision you need to make regarding the heated topic in your organization. I don't know what the topic is, so you're on your own. I will say that if you don't spend time considering both sides of the issue before you deliver, then your team will know it and your credibility will be suspect. Those on the losing side will wonder why they weren't consulted and then they'll start wandering the halls murmuring that you're either lazy or a tyrant. Ouch.

The goal of the Deliver phase is straightforward. You need to explain to the team that a decision has been made. Sounds easy, right? Well, this is where junior managers blow it. They do a good job of explaining the decision, but they fail convey that this is the decision and further debate is not necessary. A good sign of poor mandate delivery is when the delivery degrades into another debate of the issues. Delivering a mandate takes moxie. The team has got to leave the room knowing the decision has been made. They don't have to like it, they may hate it, but they can't leave the room thinking there's wiggle room in what you decided.

Again, an added benefit of my collaborative management style is that delivering mandates is less controversial because I've already vetted the various flavors of the decision with all the folks who have an opinion. When the mandate lands, it feels less like laying down the law and more like I'm relaying the results of our investigation. I still piss off those who disagree with the decision, but they know they were heard.

Deliver (Again)

Congratulations. You've delivered your first mandate and now you're staring at a room full of heads nodding in the affirmative. Even the folks who have been screwed by your decision are nodding. Well done! There's more work to do.

All that head-nodding is a big ego boost, but the fact of the matter is that each person walking out of meeting has one of three distinct opinions:

- **Yay:** You are a great motivator. The winners will have this opinion of you and you still you need to deliver (again).

- **Boo:** You are a tyrant. Commonly held by those who've been screwed. You must deliver (again).

- **Yawn:** What took you so damned long? Silent majority here. Don't sweat them.

The Deliver (Again) phase might be better called damage control, but that makes it sound like you screwed up by pushing the team forward and you didn't. Maybe. Delivering (again) is taking the time to individually express your reasoning to the concerned parties—both the winners and the losers. This not only gives you a chance to reenforce what you mandated, but also gives coworkers the chance to respond in a non-team setting. Expect more venting. In fact, insist on it. If you're sitting with someone who was on the losing side of the decision and they're still nodding their head, *they don't believe the battle is over*. They're sitting there figuring out their next move to erode the mandate. If you fail to get this person to open up, you will be mandating (again) in a few short weeks.

Delivering (again) is not going to quench discontent in your team, but it's going to give everyone involved a chance to speak up, and that should push your management karma toward motivator and away from tyrant.

Foreign Mandates

I've been talking about the ins and outs of local mandates so far. These are situations where you are the decision maker, which gives you access to a wealth of information as well as all of the players. In any decent-sized organization, you are equally likely to be on the receiving end of foreign mandates. This is a mandate that occurs way outside of your sphere of influence.

Yes, the tables are turned. Mandates might just randomly show up and there isn't a thing you can do about it.

Guess what? The same rules mentioned previously apply, with one exception. Just like your team, you are going to have one of the three opinions (yay, boo, or yawn) regarding the mandate. Regardless of what your opinion is, you must figure out the justification behind the mandate. You might have a yawn opinion about this, but what about the rest of your team? They might hate the mandate, and you are going to look lame when you relay the mandate without a clue as to why the mandate showed up.

Here's the rub—mandate justification often does not travel well through a large organization. Either someone in your management food chain had a yawn reaction to the mandate and didn't bother to gather a justification, or the grapevine has tainted the justification to the point that it no longer makes any sense. Either way, you're going to be delivering news to your team sans reasoning. This blows. I'm certain that companies that exhibit this poor communication structure are the same ones that have reputations for notoriously tyrannical CEOs. Maybe they're not tyrants. Maybe they're surrounded by poor communicators. Or maybe they are tyrants. I can't tell from where I'm sitting.

The good news is that if you ever have to deliver a mandate without the facts to back it up, you're less likely to pull a rookie mistake and land your local mandate without the reasoning . . . the justification. You're also not going to forget to deliver (again), because you know that each time you stand in front of your team, trying to be a leader, they are watching and they are listening. They want to know if you deserve the title of manager.

Information Starvation

There's someone standing outside your office and he's not saying a thing.

It's a freakout, but for now he's just standing there. Or maybe he's not. Maybe he's employing the Hover where he walks by every few minutes. Then there's the Long Stare where he stands outside and just glares. My favorite is the Avalanche, when you look up from your screen and have mere seconds to brace yourself before the tumbling heap of frustration piles into your office.

What you call these freakouts is unimportant. What's essential is that you figure out how you, the manager, could have prevented them.

Information Conduit

One of your many jobs as manager is information conduit, and the rules are deceptively simple: for each piece of information you see, you must correctly determine who on your team needs that piece of information to do their job.

Easy, right? An e-mail shows up, you read it, and decide it needs to go to one of your developers, so you forward it. Here's the wrinkle: there's vastly more information than you think; there are more people who need it than you expect; you're going to screw up your assessment of who needs it more often than not; and you've got a lot of other essential crap to do.

First, let's worry about the consequences of poor information management, because that's how I'm going to get your attention.

So, not-so-average day at the office. There are rumors of layoffs wandering the hallway and the rumors are correct. Now, Long Stare is outside your office, and, of course, the first thing you do is invite her in so you can triage the Long Stare issue.

"Why the long stare?"

"The what?"

[Denial.]

"You've been outside my office for two minutes staring at me."

"I have?"

[Wow, total denial.]

"So, what's up?"

"Um, am I going to be fired?"

Now, this is your best developer. She's your rock star. She's the one you throw the vaguest of ideas at and you know she'll turn that hand-waving into a feature, a product. She's done it *five times* and now she's in your office wondering if she's about to be fired.

What happened? How is it possible your single most valuable engineer believes she's so irrelevant that she could be let go?

She's starved. She's starved for information, and in the absence of information, people will create their own.

Nature Abhors a Vacuum

Think back to your last layoff. What happened? Well, first you heard the rumor that "layoffs are coming," which, as it turns out, wasn't a rumor and was the last factual thing you heard for the next three weeks.

See, the management team was spending those three weeks trying to figure out what's going to happen and who's going to get laid off, but they don't actually know yet so they're not saying anything, which is precisely the wrong thing to do.

Everyone else is wondering whether they have a job or not, and in the absence of knowledge, they're going to make some pretty crazy shit up. It's the rumor mill, it's the grapevine, and its existence is directly related to how well you, the manager, are communicating.

The creation of information is the act of creating context and foundation when there is none. Call it a rumor or gossip, but what it really is is a reaction to a failure to communicate. When I hear a fantastic piece of gossip, I'm listening for two things. First, what is actually being said, and second, what informational gap in knowledge is being filled by this fantastic fabrication.

Back to the rock star who thinks she's about to be fired. Given that I know there is no chance she's about to be fired, what am I hearing? First, I'm hearing, "I don't know where I stand in the organization." It's not that she actually thinks she's going to be fired—she doesn't understand her value. Second, I'm hearing, "Given that I don't know my value, I'm going to make up a crazy consequence, which isn't actually likely, but boy, will it get someone's attention."

Gossip, rumors, whatever the creation is, it means that someone, somewhere in your organization is asking for help.

Starvation Prevention

You're going to need damage control with the rock star. You're going to need to sit her down and remind her of the five different times she created great products out of your hand-waving. You're going to need to check in multiple times to make sure she know she's valued, but mostly, you're going to need to figure out how she got starved in the first place.

Well, it started with you not conveying information, we know that, but the question is, why? Here are some common failures.

"Don't worry, I'll remember to pass that on."

Perhaps the biggest loss of essential information is when managers rely on their brains as to-do lists. This is a common mistake made by green managers who haven't figured out their conduit gig yet. They sit in a meeting and hear a to-do they need to pass on to one of their engineers and they think, "Got it. Remind Bob that Phil is going to break the build unless X happens. I can remember that."

If that was the only item on the list, this manager would be in good shape, except he's got four more meetings and ten other to-dos to remember before he sees Bob in the hallway and remembers, "Phil . . . something."

Write it down. Keep a notebook with you all the time and anything that sounds remotely interesting goes in that notebook. This leads us to . . .

"I don't think anyone needs to know that."

Bill was a new manager on my team and he was just happy to be attending the staff meeting. My staff meetings are broken into two parts. Part one is the recital of all the information I've gotten from my boss's staff meeting combined with my thoughts and opinions. Part two is quick status and relevant bits from each of the folks in the team.

There was a lot of redundancy in part one. How are products doing, who has been promoted, what were the latest customer wins. If you listened to it each week, you'd be bored, but I recite the same thing. Every week.

Bill picked up on the boring immediately and stopped taking notes during part one. When I asked him, he said, "I don't think my team cares about customer wins for a product they're not responsible for."

"Really? Why don't you ask them?"

The following week Bill was furiously taking notes. His comment: "Yeah, they want to hear it all."

Especially in larger organizations, you need to pay careful attention to maintaining a consistent flow of organization information. It might feel like you're passing on useless information, but the rule of thumb is that you never know what your team is going to care about. I had an engineer who faithfully kept a running diary of who our new customers were, and, after a few months, he knew more about our customer base than most of our sales folks.

I realize it could be a full-time job relaying every piece of information that you're exposed to, and part of your job as a manager is to make judgment calls regarding what gets passed on. My rule of thumb is that if I'm debating whether to pass something on for more than a few seconds, I might not be qualified to decide, so pass it on and see what happens.

"My employees can read my mind."

Maybe you're doing a good job of relaying information. You've got content-rich staff meetings and a steady flow of forwarded e-mails. That's terrific. I'm glad you're passing on all the information, but the question is, "What are your employees hearing?"

The last VP at the startup did a stunning job of forwarding every single e-mail that showed up in his inbox. Every e-mail. It was great to be included in all the VP's communications, but it was a borderline spam situation. What was worse was his cryptic brief additions to the beginning of each e-mail.

"Interesting."

"We should."

"Hah. Told you!"

More often than not, I could dereference his one-word thoughts based on recent conversations, but there were times I had no clue what I was supposed to do with an e-mail.

Simply because an e-mail or thought makes sense or has some interesting context in your head doesn't automatically mean the insight is going to be obvious to anyone else. It's a goal of mine to have a team that is working closely enough together that they share a common mind, but taking the time to give each piece of information that you're passing on a bit of your personal context never hurts. It takes time, but it maintains the quality of the information while preventing a slow mutation into confusion.

The good news is, if you're ever wondering what your team heard or read when you pass on your information, you can ask one of my favorite follow-up questions: "What did you just hear?"

Aggressive Silence

A structured regimen of information dispersion is the first step in keeping the team in touch with the rest of the organization, but you're still going to screw up. Whether it's one of the failures I described previously or a totally different failure, your job is to constantly assess what your team needs, and I've got really good news.

Your team is going to tell you what they need. Whether it's gossip, rumors, staring, pacing, or yelling, your team is always telling you what they need to know. This means your job is not just to be an information conduit; it's also to employ a policy of aggressive silence. In this silence, you're going to be forced to listen. Try it in a staff meeting; just shut up and see what your team says when you're saying nothing.

Subtlety, Subterfuge, and Silence

Managers, wannabe managers, and folks who want to understand managers simply need to read *The 48 Laws of Power*, by Robert Greene and Joost Elffers.

I've purposely not done any background research on this document because my first reaction to this list was profound and I wanted to stare at that reaction. There's some pretty evil shit documented there as well as some basic truths about what managers are up to on a daily basis. I can't tell if the guys who wrote this are serious when they write "Keep Others in Suspended Terror: Cultivate an Air of Unpredictability," but after several readings, yeah, I think they're serious.

My problem with this list and how it relates to managers is that so many of the "rules" involve psychological torture of those you're trying to lead, and that strikes me as a good way to further the intense negative knee-jerk reaction regarding managers. "That guy is a power-hungry jerk."

Still.

Part of management is navigating your way through some tricky political jungles. Part of management is getting folks to comfortably bend in an uncomfortable direction. A good manager is a person who is playing to a strategy and isn't merely stumbling around squashing fires all day.

Management is chess. When you're presented with a problem, you sometimes need to sit back and take a look at the board, figure out the consequences of each of move, and, most importantly, pick a move. In my experience, the move and how you pick it does not involve 48 laws, it's only 3 words: subtlety, subterfuge, and silence.

Subtlety

Worst performance review ever. I've just delivered a painful performance review to a fictional employee and he doesn't get it. Two weeks I spent writing this thing, gathering different perspectives from peer feedback, rereading relevant e-mails from the past year, and rewriting, rewriting, and rewriting. He's sitting there like everything's dandy.

I'm not about to fire this guy, but given his current trajectory, he's two years from becoming irrelevant and I want to nip this in the bud, but it's radio silence.

"Any questions on your review?"

"Nope."

"Are you clear about the areas I want to work with you on?"

"Yup."

Now, the point of a performance review has nothing to do with the review, it's the conversation. It's about constructively conveying information about the performance of the coworker and then chewing on it a bit. You want to see the person is processing the information you just presented; you want them to ask questions.

Nothing.

OK, so maybe the performance review wasn't the right place to course correct. Maybe I need to use a subtler approach. A week later, we were in our one-on-one and I had a list. It had each and every discussion point I had for this gentleman rewritten to support the areas of improvement I called out in the performance review.

The employee in question wasn't comfortable with the strategic broadstrokes I'd painted in the review, but when I carefully mapped the review into our tactical day-to-day work, he was listening. By the end of the one-on-one, I'd piled his to-do list so high, we were actually back talking about the performance review because it was that advice that was going to help him get the work done.

Subtlety starts with humility. It starts with admitting that you're not going to have all the answers as a manager and giving yourself time to carefully consider your response. I know it feels great to make that snap decision and show the team you're the guy in charge, but was it the right decision or was it ego?

Subtlety finishes with elegance. It's not just successfully solving whatever hard problem you're staring at, it's that you solve it in an ingenious novel way that builds and refines your management aptitude.

Subterfuge

Say it with me: "sub-ter-fyoooooooooj." We should make shirts, it's that fun to say, but what does it mean? *Subterfuge* means "intrigue, deviousness, deceit, deception, dishonesty, cheating, duplicity, guile, cunning, craftiness, chicanery, pretense, fraud, fraudulence." Those definitions cover a lot of territory, so let's refine it for the sake of this piece.

Relative to management, this does not mean "deceit, dishonesty, cheating, fraud, or fraudulence" . . . it's everything else. I'll explain.

We were at a crossroads at the startup. Too much to do, two vastly different directions in which the team wanted to head. There were the infrastructure folks who wanted to spend three months replacing the application server and then there were the interaction folks who wanted to improve the usability of the application. The VP listened to both sides and then he decided, "Infrastructure! Long-term scalability!"

The interaction folks were pissed. Their response: "Who cares about long-term scalability if no one wants to use the product?" Oh yeah, I was also the manager of the interaction folks and I agreed with them, but I had to throw my engineers on the infrastructure work because we didn't have the capacity. I was talking with existing customers and they weren't pulling their hair out because the application was sluggish, but rather because it was an interaction nightmare. They were spending most of their time trying to figure the damned thing out.

Grrrrrrrr.

The lead interaction designer, an engineer, and I sat in a conference room fuming in silence when it popped into my head: "Hey, people are visual creatures, how long to throw together a prototype that shows off what we were thinking?"

My engineer: "A week!" Good time to point out how enthusiasm reduces all engineering estimates by a third. My engineer continued, "But I'll need Frank."

Hmmmmm.

"Here's what we're going to do. I want you and Frank to work on this after 5 p.m., after we're done with our infrastructure work, and I want you to keep this on the down low. If, after a week, we like what we see, we're going public."

Herein lies the hard part of subterfuge. Depending on where you are standing, my plan could be viewed in any number of ways. The other engineering director would have called it "disobeying a direct order," whereas my boss, who got wind of the effort two days in, called it "a skunk works project" and told us to proceed. Phew.

Our skunk works took us three weeks, not one, but when we showed off our work, the VP of engineering and VP of marketing were impressed and wanted to see us finish the work. Rather than sacrificing the infrastructure effort, they gave me two requisitions so I could hire a team to do the job right.

Subterfuge is a risk. The infrastructure director never quite trusted me after that even though I still went out of my way to keep him in the loop after we went public with our work.

The use of subterfuge for good means keeping the intent honest. If you're going commando to do what you believe is right, it doesn't mean someone isn't going to be pissed, but it should allow you to sleep at night.

Silence

Your most annoying employee sits across the table and he's on a roll. This guy is a total and complete personality clash with you and he's in his second hour of rambling about something you don't understand. My advice is simple:

Shut up.

I mean it.

Now, if you know what he's trying to get at and you've continued to let him blather, OK, you can start talking and directing him elsewhere, but if he's valiantly trying to get to the point, you must shut up and listen. Your silence is giving him a chance to get something out.

I'm not a fan of public speaking. I'm not comfortable with the all-hands meeting where I'm laying out the next six months of work. My natural state is one of introspection where I'm soaking in the world, and the skill has taken me far because so many folks out there just can't shut up. While all this talking is going on, I sit quietly and nod while learning what all these yammering people are about and carefully file it away for future reference.

Managers lead, and a lot of managers translate that into "managers lead by talking." Combined with the tendency of employees to not say no to these managers, you can see why a lot of us have turned into professional windbags. We think we're guiding you by filling the air with our thoughts. There's a time and place for that, but in order to fill the air with something relevant, you've got to gather and process data.

In silence, you can assess.

My favorite use of silence is a huge cross-functional meeting with a group I've never worked with before where I have no role other than listener. It's a table full of people I don't know and I feel like I'm sitting at the worst poker table ever because everyone tells you what they got.

Remember this: in most businesses, everyone's basic agenda is visible after they've talked for about 30 seconds. I'm not talking about who they are as a person, I'm talking about figuring out what they have and what they need. In poker, you keep this information hidden as best you can because your money is on the line. In business, everyone throws their hand on the table, stands up, points at their hand, and says, "People, I'm one card away from the nut flush. Who's going to give the queen of hearts?"

Asking for what you need is a good strategy in business; it's called collaborating. Each time I hear "I need," I learn another bit about those I work with and, in time, I can construct a better picture of how to interact with my coworkers. Still, I'm also wondering about that guy in the corner who isn't saying a thing. His eyes are darting around the room just like mine and I'm curious . . . what is he getting out of his silence?

Business Isn't War

The "48 laws of power" are the real deal, but they are focused on war, not business. Go buy the book if you want to know more, but read wisely. With each successful year on the job, I find myself adjusting to the ever-increasing complexity with which my peers play the game of management. Fifteen years in, I can safely say there is one law that is true: if you're only interested in building power, you're going to lose.

Managementese

One of my teams is facing a big, fat decision regarding future product direction, and the process has split the team in half: the Yes We Shoulds and the No Way in Hells. The manager of the team is facing a rebellion and spending much of his time trying to drive the team toward a decision.

I walked by his office and he was talking with one of the No Way in Hells, trying to influence them over to the other side of the fence. I overheard a blurb of his conversation, "I think it's a key decision and I'm asking you to think outside of the box . . ."

I cringed.

Management speak.

Walking back to my office, I thought about my negative reaction to the term "outside of the box." What does that actually mean? Well, it means something like "Don't restrict your thinking to conventional avenues," but that's not what your team hears when you say it. They hear, "Hi, I'm a manager, and as a manager I'm telling you that you should be creative without actually telling you how to be creative."

No, that's not right. What they hear is, "Hi, I'm a manager and I've stopped thinking and I'm using throwaway phrases that obscure what I mean."

And managers wonder why no one trusts them.

As I sat in my office, a project manager came in for a one-on-one. With the observation fresh in my mind, I attempted to monitor all my usage of managementese during our half-hour meeting. Here are my offenses:

"Can you *circle back* with her . . ."

"I want to *double-click* on that and . . ."

"These are the *action items* . . ."

What I learned: I've turned into a total dorkwad manager and can no longer communicate like a normal human being.

Management Metaphors

One of my favorite books on software construction is Steve McConnell's *Code Complete*. In the second chapter, McConnell describes the richness of language around computer science: "Computer Science has some of the most colorful language of any field. In what other field can you walk into a sterile room, carefully controlled at 68 degrees Fahrenheit and find viruses, Trojan horses, worms, bugs, bombs, crashes, flames, twisted sex changers, and fatal errors."

He continues: "A software metaphor is more like a searchlight than a road map. It doesn't tell you where to find the answer, it tells you how to look for it."

I'd always assumed that management metaphors fell into the same bucket, and they do, but if your team doesn't know what you're talking about, you might as well be speaking in code.

Managementese is the language that is learned, evolved, and spoken by managers. For communication between managers, it's a convenient, high-bandwidth means of conveying information. Chances are, when you say "double-click" to a fellow manager, they understand that you are suggesting that they should pay attention to whatever it is you're doing.

There are unique spheres of language that exist in each part of the corporate organizational chart. Inside of each sphere is the language that is unique to the job. Engineers have one, marketing has another, and sales has yet another. In each of these groups, there are the managers who must speak their native language, as well as be able to translate between spheres in order to get the job done. I believe this is a legitimate reason for managementese. It's the cross-functional language of the company. Without it, the different parts of the organization aren't going to be able to communicate with each other.

Managers are hubs of communication. The better they communicate across these sphere boundaries, the more people they can communicate with, and the more data they have, which consequently leads to better decision-making. Ultimately, stronger communicators make more informed decisions, and hopefully are more successful because they waste less time wondering what to do.

Still, when you say "double-click" to an employee, they do know what you're talking about, but they also know that you've just self-identified as a manager. Why didn't you just say what you actually meant? My first guess is that you're in a hurry, but that's not what your team is hearing.

Language of the Lazy

In high tech, we're all in an incredible fucking hurry. We're working against an unreasonable deadline and we're over-committed on features. As a manager, your job is that of bullshit umbrella. You need to decide what crap your team needs to deal with and what crap can be ignored. That means that you need to rapidly acquire information from a variety of people. In that rush, manage-mentese can help you talk with your fellow managers to figure out what the hell is going on, but you're only half done. You still need to communicate to your team.

This can be tiresome because you, of all people, are absolutely sure what you're saying. This is why you might be tempted to use the readily accessible management metaphor–laced language that you're familiar with. Don't.

The main issue folks have with managementese is not that they don't understand what is being said; their issue is that they don't trust it. Think of the worst all-hands meeting you've ever been at and tell me why you hated it.

"Management is out of touch with what we're doing."

"They're all talk and no action."

"He's talking in generalities and what I want is specifics."

"He sure sounds like he believes what he's saying, but I don't know what he's saying."

Managers in a hurry need to remember that managementese is a few key metaphors away from sounding like a used car salesmen. Talking fast with confidence might feel like you're getting something done, but if the people you are talking to don't trust you, they're never going to understand what you're saying.

My advice is simple: when you're talking to individuals, talk to them using the familiar language of a friend. Dispose of the management hat and have a conversation. This takes practice in a busy day because the disposal of the management hat is a major context switch for you, but your goal is to have a conversation, and for that to happen, both people sitting at the table need to trust and understand what is being said.

Ninety-five percent of the people in a big company simply have no clue what corporate machinations are going down and how they might be affected and whether or not they'll be working in the next six months. How you will be judged as a manager by your team is based on how you communicate with them. That's not just taking the time to have that quarterly all-hands, it's understanding what they need to hear and being able to say it in a way they'll understand.

Technicality

There's a very short list of new manager "must-dos" in the Rands Management Rule Book. The brevity of this list comes from the fact that a must is an absolute and, when it comes to people, there are very few absolutes. A clever way to manage one person is a disaster when applied to another. This makes the first item on the management must-do list:

Stay flexible.

The only constant in management is that believing you've seen it all is a bad idea. Staying flexible is the only stance to adopt when constant change is the only constant.

Paradoxically, the second item on the list is surprisingly inflexible and it's still a personal favorite of mine because I believe it helps set the stage for management growth. It reads:

Stop coding.

The theory is this: if you want to be a manager, you must learn to trust those who work for you to take care of the job of coding. This advice can be hard to digest, especially for new managers. It's likely that one of the reasons they became managers is due to their productive developers, and their first reaction when things go to crap is to revert to the skills that built up their confidence. That's writing code.

When I see a new manager fall back to coding, I tell the manager, "I know you can code. The question is, can you manage? You're no longer responsible for yourself, you're responsible for the team, and I want to see you figure out how to get the team to solve this problem without you coding. Your job is to figure out how to get yourself to scale. I want lots of you, not just one."

Good advice, huh? Scale, management, and responsibility. Very buzzword-compliant. Too bad I'm wrong.

Wrong?

Yup. Wrong. Not totally, but enough that I might need to make some calls to past coworkers and apologize. "That 'stop coding' pitch of mine? Wrong. Yeah. Start programming again. Start with Python or Ruby. Yeah. I mean it. Your career depends on it."

When I began my career as a developer at Borland, I was part of the Paradox for Windows team, and this was a big one. Just on the application development team we had 13 developers. If you included the heads from the various other teams who provided essential technology like the core database engine, graphing engine, and core application services, you're talking 50 engineers directly contributing to the product.

No team that I've been on since then has even been close in terms of size. In fact, with each passing year, the size of the engineering teams contributing to my products has steadily shrunk. What's going on? Are we getting collectively smarter as developers? Nope, we're just distributing the load.

What have we, as developers, been doing for the past 20 years? Well, we've been writing a crap load of code. Piles of it. So much of it that we decided that maybe it was a good idea to make it easy to share by open sourcing it. Thankfully the Internet showed up, which made this sharing trivial. If you're a developer, try this right now. Go search Google Code for your name and find some code you forgot about that everyone can see. Scary, huh? Didn't think your code lived forever? It does.

Code lives forever. Good code not only lives, it grows as those who value it make sure that it doesn't become stale. It's this pile of high-value, well-maintained code that is helping shrink the average size of the engineering team because it's allowing us to focus less on writing new code and more on integrating existing code to get the job done with fewer people and in less time.

There's a depressing line of reasoning here, the idea that we're all just a bunch of integration automatons using duct tape to connect different preexisting moving parts to create slightly different versions of the same thing. It's this train of thought that has a lot of senior management teams excited about outsourcing. "Anyone who can use Google and has some duct tape can do this, so why are we paying big bucks for our local automatons?"

We're paying these management types some pretty big bucks to think this crap up. Still, it brings up my final point that there are eager, bright developers all over the planet and they're eager and bright even though they haven't spent a moment in an accredited university. Oh yeah, and there lots more of them coming.

I'm not suggesting that you should be worried about your job because some bright fellow overseas is gunning for you, I'm suggesting that you should be worried about your job because the evolution of how software development occurs might be moving faster than you. You've been working for ten years in your job, five years as a manager, and you're thinking, "I know how to develop software." And you do. Right now.

Stop Coding?

If you follow my advice and remove yourself from the code, then you are removing yourself from the act of creation. This act is why I don't really sweat outsourcing. Automatons don't build, they process. While good process can save a lot of money, it's not going to bring anything new to the world.

With smaller teams doing more for less, removing yourself from the code strikes me as a bad career move. Even in a monstrous company laden with policy, process, and politics, you can't forget how to develop software. And how to develop software is changing. Now. Right under your feet, this very second.

You have issues. I understand. Let's hear them.

"Rands, I'm on the director track, and if I keep coding, no one is going to think I can scale."

My first question to you is this: from where you are sitting in your soon-to-be-director chair, do you see software development changing within your company? If the answer is yes, my next question is: how is it changing, and what are you going to do about it? If your answer is no, then you need to move your chair because, I swear to you, software development is changing right this second. How in the world are you going to scale if you're slowly forgetting how software is made?

My advice is not that you start assigning yourself tons of features in the next release. My advice is that you take action so that you stay in touch with how your team builds stuff. You can do this as a director or a VP. More on this in a moment.

"Uh, Rands, someone has to referee. Someone has to have the vision. If I code, I'm going to lose perspective on my job."

You still need to referee, you still need to massage decisions, and you still need to spend 30 minutes every Monday morning walking around the block four times with that engineer who needs to walk through his weekly "we're doomed" rant, but you also need to lose perspective about your job and you do not need to be a full-time coder to do this.

My advice for losing perspective:

1. Use the development environment to build the product. This means you must be familiar with your team's tools, including the build system, version control, and programming language. This task is going to keep you in touch with the language your team uses to talk about how they get stuff done. And it will also allow you to continue to use your favorite text editor . . . which rocks.

2. Be able to draw a detailed architectural diagram describing your product on any whiteboard at any time. I'm not talking about the three-boxes-and-two-arrows versions. You need to know the detailed one, the hard one that isn't pretty and is tricky to explain. This is your map for understanding just about everything about your product. It changes over time and you should be able to understand why those changes are occurring.

3. Own a feature. I'm literally cringing as I write this because it is fraught with danger, but I don't think you can really do #1 or #2 without a feature that is yours. Owning a feature not only forces you to actively participate in the development process, it also switches your context from "manager responsible for everything" to "person who owns a thing." This is a humble, unassuming perspective that will remind you about the importance of small decisions.

I'm still cringing. Someone is already yelling at me, *"Managers owning features??!?!"* (And I agree.) You are still a manager, so make it a small feature, OK? You've still got a lot to do. If you can't imagine owning a feature, my backup advice is to fix some bugs. You won't get the joy of ownership, but you'll gain an understanding of the construction of the product that you'll never get walking the hallway.

4. Write a test script. I still do this late in the product cycle when folks are losing their minds. This is a simple script that you run with each build. Think of it as your checklist for understanding what your product does. Show it to coworkers. Do it often.

"Rands, if I code, I'm going to confuse my team. They're not going to know if I'm a manager or a developer."

Good.

I mean it. I'm happy you're about to confuse your team by swimming in the developer pool. The simple fact is that well-defined roles in software development are fading. User interface guys are doing what can only be called development in JavaScript and CSS. Developers are learning more about interaction design. Everybody is talking to everybody else and they're learning from each other's mistakes, stealing each other's code, and there is no reason that a manager shouldn't be participating in this massive global cross-pollination information cluster-fuck.

Besides, you want to be a part of a team of interchangeable parts. Not only does this make your team more nimble, it presents each person with the opportunity to see the product and the company from a vastly different perspective. How much more are you going to respect quiet Frank the Build Guy when you see the simple elegance of his build scripts?

I'm not wishing confusion and chaos on your team. I'm actually wishing better communication on it. My belief is that if you are building the product and touching the features, you'll be closer to your team. But, more importantly, you'll be closer to how software development is constantly changing in your organization.

One Absolute

A coworker at Borland once verbally assaulted me for calling her a coder.

"Rands, a coder is mindless machine. A monkey. A coder does nothing relevant except lay down boring lines of useless code. I am a software developer."

She was right and she would've hated my advice for new managers to stop coding. Not because I was suggesting that they were coders, but more that I was proactively telling them to start ignoring one of the most important parts of their jobs: software development.

So, I've revised my advice. You can stop coding, but . . .

Stay flexible and don't stop developing.

Avoiding the Fez

Fez.

Fez is a senior engineer who works for me. He's fictional, but you know Fez. He's the guy who wrote that piece of code 9 million years ago that everyone is dependent on, but no one knows what exactly it does because Fez didn't bother to comment a single line . . . oh yeah, and he wrote it in Forth.

Fez has his own office and he nods a lot. It's the nod of a man who believes he's got rock-solid job security because his technology is critical. Fez bugs a lot of people, but when it hits the fan, Fez saves the day because he's carefully cordoned off a critical path that is his and his alone.

Each year, Fez and I sit down and I present his focal review. I set the stage by asking about his aspirations and he responds with vague nodding.

Sounds good, boss.

OK, boss.

Sure, boss.

Fez is not hearing a word of our discussion because Fez has heard this focal review mumbo jumbo for 12 years straight. He believes he's immune.

The approach of the Fez is a rock-solid way to slowly become irrelevant and, more importantly, become unemployed.

Understanding Where You Stand

The definition of a healthy business is a business that is growing, and by growing I mean it is making more money each year. There's a plethora of different ways that a company can create this growth, but the basic law of business physics that you should never forget is "As a business grows, so shall its employees."

The manner by which a business prunes the employees who aren't assisting in this growth is horrifically efficient. First, we have the employees who have consistently demonstrated an inability or lack of interest in helping with this growth. Their prize is the irrelevant project that no one cares about. Some folks find this banishment to be comforting. "Aaaahh . . . no more fire drills . . . the execs don't even care about this project, so I can cruise." That's right. They don't care about that particular division because it's not strategic, which means the moment it's time to tighten the budgetary belt that is the first group to be nuked. Poof. Welcome to unemployment. Did you learn your lesson, yet? Probably should have taken the time to figure out what XML stood for.

Then we have Fez. Maybe he's grown complacent with the knowledge that he's the only person who has a particular skill or set of knowledge. It's a powerful position to be in . . . for a while.

Maybe the execs won't fire him because of the perception he has essential knowledge, but, I guarantee, those who are dependent on his black box of knowledge are concocting a devious plan to replace him and his knowledge because *they want to grow*. Right this second, three guys down the hall have rewritten Fez's code in C and they're secretly demonstrating their work to interested parties. They are building support, they are building a revolution, and they're not going to stop until the person who is hindering their growth is gone.

Whether it's by organizational evolution or revolution, complacency is a job killer, and if you're following me, you think Fez has blown it.

Wrong.

I did.

I blew it by not convincing Fez that growth is life.

Getting Started

Let's start with the bad news. There's no silver bullet to solve the Fez issue. Solving Fez is going to involve strategy, effort, inspiration, luck, and, lastly, a bit of time. You won't solve it in a moment and you won't solve it in a meeting.

There is a convenient yearly inflection point where everyone panics about their careers. Annual reviews. I'm going to construct this article around annual reviews, but I don't want you to think that performing an annual review will solve the Fez. If you worry about career development once a year, you're screwed. As you'll see, avoiding the Fez is a full-time job, but since you get actual allocated time to stress about employee development, why not stress in a constructive manner?

Annual Reviews, Briefly

People do care about cash. When that annual review begins, your employee is hanging on every word, carefully listening to your tone, wondering, good review or bad review? If it's sounding good, that must mean cash; and cash rocks. If it's sounding bad, they stop listening and start pre-bittering themselves for hating you for the next month since you clearly have *no idea* where they *added their value* this year.

Compensation adjustments are the reward everyone cares about, but does anyone actually know how they're calculated? What happened over the previous 365 days to result in a *big cash windfall* or an *insignificant pittance*?

If you don't draw a concrete line between a coherent understanding of an employee's performance and their reward or punishment, you are only adding more fuel to the argument that "managers sit around doing nothing all day." Let's begin . . .

First, Gather Your Thoughts, But Don't Think (Yet)

Here's the deal. If I asked you right this second to tell me about your particular local Fez, you've already got a strong opinion, but it's an opinion of the moment. It's the last three interactions you've had with your Fez, and while those are relevant, they hardly represent a complete picture of a year of work.

When you're assessing an employee, you need to assess against their job, not the work they've done over the past two months. This is hard because this is the Silicon Valley and no one knows what happened two months ago. *Google bought YouTube then Christmas then iPhone, right? Did I miss anything important? Is Leopard out yet?*

You did. Every month, your team produced something and it's your job to document that production. I do this by spending an hour a month jotting down reflections of the team for the past 30 days. What stands out in my mind? What'd we do? Who rocked? Don't get hung up on documenting every single event or talking about every single person . . . just type. Even if you miss massive contributions by a team member, the act of capturing your thoughts at the time they were happening creates a handy mental bookmark. This bookmark captures not only what you wrote, but everything else hiding around it. When you go back and read last summer's terribly small entry:

"This month blew. No time to write."

You'll not only remember that you were on a death march, but you'll also remember that Eddie the QA guy was there with you that weekend and, oh hey, he's been here every single weekend and, wow, why aren't we promoting him?

Regular snapshots of your team's work will construct an impression of your team that you are incapable of constructing in the moment because, in the moment, you're cranky about not getting coffee this morning, stressed about your product review next week, and *don't get me started about the 300 mails I have yet to read.* How can you create an objective opinion of someone's performance with all this crap in your head? You gotta step back, take a deep breath, and reflect.

As you sit there staring at the ceiling chewing on a year of thoughts, an overall impression is going to form . . . you can't avoid it, but I'm asking you to ignore it for now. I'm going to distract you by proposing a model that you can use to look at your employees and begin to understand what exactly their career needs. The model is Skill vs. Will.

Skill vs. Will Plus Epiphanies

It's a simple graph. One axis is skill—how much skill does the employee have to do their job? Are they qualified? Overqualified? How long have they been doing it? When is the last time you know they learned something new? How quickly do they handle tasks compared to their peers?

The other axis is will—this is where we measure the employee's desire. Do they like their job? Really? Have they told you that? Are they viewed as energetic by their team? When is the last time they generated a great idea that blew your mind? Are they talking in meetings or listening? Are they *ever* talking? Are they *always* talking?

This graph is not a precision instrument. It's a tool to better define the impression you're constructing of your employee. Once you've placed someone on the Skill/Will graph, you can begin to consider what your full-time job is—constantly and consistently pushing your employees to the upper-right quadrant. High skill (I'm good at what I do) and high will (I like what I do). This mental map is the first step in constructing a Fez-avoidance insurance policy.

"Rands, um, what exactly am I pushing constantly and consistently?"

Great question.

Worst-case scenario. You've ignored everything I've said so far. You're spending 15 days rereading your Fez's review from last year. Then, you spend another 15 throwing together this year's review by cutting and pasting the one and only review you wrote for all your employees, making it unique by inserting their full name and project name. Dear lord. You've really blown it.

Yet, you haven't fully blown it. A complete fuck-up is when you take this pathetic excuse for a review and present it. You say, "Employee 629, here is your review. You did this well, you did this poorly. Here's your 2 percent increase and here's your indecipherable objectives for next year. *Back to work.*"

You deserve every single Fez that you get. Please stop reading, pack your things, and quietly exit the Silicon Valley. Thanks.

If you've taken some time to reflect on the full year, if you've mapped your employee against skill and will, you've probably had some epiphany regarding the Fez. You've realized, "Wow, they're bored," or "She really has no clue how to architect software." Great, an epiphany . . . it's a start, but it's not a finish.

You are not the one who needs to have the epiphany. It's your employee who needs it.

I'll explain via the real fictional Fez. Go back and think about where you'd put him on the Skill/Will graph. Your gut might say, well, he's worked a lot of years, so he's high skill and he's just bored, so he's low will.

Nice try, but you don't have the 12 months of fictional notes that I have. See, Fez's skill used to be high, but it's fading. It's middle-of-the-road skill now and the slow erosion is also affecting his confidence . . . his will. His diminishing skill is diminishing his will, which, in turn, further diminishes his skill because he has zero confidence to go gather new skills. Yikes. A skill/will negative feedback loop. Didn't see that coming, did you?

Here's the upside. Just as skill and will fade together, they also rise together. If you focus on one, you often fix the other. It's a brilliant management two-for-one.

Back to Fez. Let's say your epiphany is to get Fez some technical training. Send him to a C++ class and *wham*, he's going to be happy. *Hurry*, write that down as an objective because *wow*, you've really nailed that Fez problem.

Easy, eager manager. Slow down.

Assertiveness, Briefly

I've got a task for you and I'm going to ask you in two different ways. You tell me which request you're going to actually do:

- **Request #1:** You—go fix that bug.
- **Request #2:** Hey, can you look into bug #1837?

The difference between these two requests is a management style that shows up in every personality test. You, Mr. Manager, are either *ask assertive*, meaning that you ask in order to get stuff done, or *tell assertive*, which means you tell to make progress.

There are a great many charismatic leaders who've made billions by only telling folks what to do. I am not one of them. It's not that I'm conflict averse or that there are not times that I'm an incessant dictator, it's merely I hate being told what to do, so I treat others like I'd prefer to be treated.

Telling your Fez what the problem is without belief on their part that a problem exists is tantamount to a personal attack. "You, Fez, are doing a poor job and I've decided that objectives x, y, and z are the only way that we're going to save your job."

I exaggerate for example, but I've had ten-plus years of reviews and I've had some phenomenal managers turn a review into a speech about me without involving me. Well, I happen to be an expert about me, so can I please be involved in the discussion?

An annual review is a discussion, not a speech. The goal of the discussion is to, first, agree that the review is in the ballpark. Remember, you've been thinking about the review for weeks because you've got a deadline. Fez is seeing it for the first time and he needs time to mentally digest. It's very hard to be mentally nimble when your manager is staring you down asking, "Any questions?" It's doubly hard when they've just told you that you screwed up for the past year.

Rule of thumb: If you're delivering big bad news, schedule two meetings. At the first meeting, you're presenting the review, not the objectives. They're going to want to know about compensation and you're going to want to say it, but don't. The moment you say "No increase," the review is over, the employee is pissed, and you're going to be on the defensive. The meeting has become a mental fight and fights only prove who can punch harder.

It's the second meeting where everyone involved has had time to digest the review. You can have a discussion about objectives because Fez drove home the prior night wondering, "My manager is telling me that I'm getting stale and I vehemently disagree with that . . . buuuuuuuut maybe there's some truth in what he's saying . . . hmmmmmmm."

With just a smidgen of agreement that the review is fair combined with you and your Fez agreeing about his place on skill/will, you can start talking objectives. What can do we to increase skill or will? New job? New tasks? Training? Maybe move him off that team of pessimists so he can spread his wings with some optimists?

I don't know what is up with your particular Fez, so I can't advise specific objectives, but here are some high-level thoughts about the extremes on the Skill/Will graph:

- **High skill, low will:** Boredom is imminent—needs a change of scenery and responsibility. Stat.

- **High will, low skill:** Needs training, needs mentorship. Needs management. The good news is they really, really want it. Savor this because as soon as the skill kicks in, they're going to start wanting your job. This rules.

- **Low will, low skill:** Boy, did you screw up. It takes a fairly concerted effort to ignore the needs of your employee so long that (a) they no longer have the skills necessary to do their job, and (b) they don't want to do it. Roll those sleeves up, pal. You've got work to do.

- **High skill, high will:** Great job, ummmmmmm, guess what? No one stays here long.

Big Finish

Fez is career drift.

You've got some Fez in you right now. You may be the rock star of your company right now, but you have no clue that three guys in a garage in San Jose are spending every waking hour working to make you irrelevant . . . they call it the New Whizbang and you're going to hate the New Whizbang when it shows up because you know it replaces your corporate relevancy.

Your manager is not going to hate the New Whizbang because she doesn't feel personally threatened by it. She is going to see you Fezzing out about it and, hopefully, she can figure out to trickle objectivity into your indignation.

I have a simple way of managing against Fez. I tell everyone I hire the same thing: "I hired you because you've got enough skill and enough will to have my job one day . . . whether you want it or not." This statement tells those I work with that I expect them to succeed and reminds me to keep moving because there is nothing like having bright people nipping at your heels to keep you running.

Your Resignation Checklist

Borland was tanking. I'd survived three rounds of layoffs primarily because my project was still generating quite a bit of revenue, but every meeting I attended everyone kept using the word *if*.

"Well, if we get funded we'll be able to do this."

"If Paul stays, we can keep this feature."

"I don't know if this is a good idea given what we don't know."

If—everywhere. *If* is uncertainty. *If* is fear. If there were no *if*, I'd be able to focus on my job, but I couldn't because no one was sure what was going to happen.

When I finally received an offer from a database company in Redwood City, I was in bliss for a brief moment. The new company had scads of cash, upside, and a distinct lack of *if*. The bliss quickly faded when I realized I had no idea how I was going to resign. I knew it was customary to give two weeks' notice, so when the beginning of those two weeks showed up, I walked into the boss's office with my terse resignation letter and said it: "I've got another gig; I like it here, but it's time to go."

Boss: "Sorry to hear that. If I could make some changes, would you stay?"

Me: "I have a problem with your *if*."

Boss: "I understand. Well, you're responsible for the import/export engine features. Any chance you could finish that before you go?"

Me: [without pause] "*Absolutely.*"

Some data. I had four weeks of work left on the import/export engine, and those were four engineering weeks, which meant I actually had six weeks of work on the inside. While I valiantly worked my ass off for the first week, I started to not care in the second. By the time Thursday arrived, it was clear I didn't have a chance to do a third of the work.

Why did I sign up for an impossible task? I violated the first rule on the resignation checklist.

Rule #1: Don't Promise What You Can't Do

If you're resigning, you'll be tempted to over-commit on deliverables because you're leaving. This is your guilt talking. You feel bad for resigning and you are trying to make up for the fact that you're leaving people you care about in the lurch. You need to remember that, no matter how had you try, you will become useless in your final days.

It's called short timer's disease, and it begins the moment you resign. In that moment, you leave. You've got two weeks left, but you are not there. You've mentally started imagining your new job, and while you go through the motions of your old job, it's a meaningless blend of unfulfilling repetition.

Your case of short timer's disease, unfortunately, isn't strong enough when your boss asks you to finish that critical feature. Congratulations on having the moral fortitude to have the guilt about leaving, but understand that you are signing up for damaging your reputation when you agree to do work you can't complete.

Rule #2: Respect Your Network

There are, at least, three people you'll need to make sure are aware that you want to stay in touch with them. I don't know who these people are because I don't know who you are or what you do, but I know that if you don't carefully handle this transition, you're going to lose them. If you're looking for a way to identify these people, stare at your lunch crowd. Pick the ones whose meetings you care about. If you've got a folder in your inbox *just for this person*, you're going to want to make sure they know you care.

No matter where you are in your career, you need to continually develop your network of people because it's likely that one of these three people will assist in future employment or opportunity. I've been in high tech for over a decade, and every single job I've had has either been a direct or indirect result of knowing someone from a prior job. You'll hear the phrase "It's a small valley." It's a small world.

You need to go out of your way to make this happen, but it only need be a small gesture. A brief one-on-one moment where you acknowledge this person is relevant. More than a fly-by "bye" on your last day. Less than a tearful hug in the hallway.

Rule #3: Update Your Rolodex

I have a Rolodex. It's a collection of each person that I've worked with in past 15 years that I would hire if I began a startup. There are people on this list that I've failed to talk to in the past decade, but, when the startup happens,

I'm going to take the time to find them because they made the Rolodex. Each time I quit a job, I take an hour to update the Rolodex because there are always people I want to keep.

There's a good chance there is intersection between rules #2 and #3, but they are separate tasks. The people you need to actively stay in touch with are not necessarily the ones you're going to build your future company around.

Still, like rule #2, a small gesture to your new Rolodex entries is essential. Remember, you're the one who is leaving, who is changing, so it's your responsibility to create the final impression.

Rule #4: Don't Take Cheap Shots

If you aren't leaving under the best of terms, you'll be tempted to send out the scathing e-mail that sets things right. This is stupid on many levels. It will negate any positive work that you did while you were with the company. You'll also hurt your network because everyone (including those who know that you aren't insane) will remember you as that whack job that freaked out in e-mail and didn't bother to spell check.

Remember, you are leaving and the people you consider to be the problem are staying. It's not your problem anymore, don't waste your energy.

We had a B– QA engineer at the startup who got passed over for a promotion and decided to bail in style. One the last day of his employment, he sent a grammatically painful e-mail that went through his organization, person by person, and hammered them. His incoherent rambling was posted on the cube walls for its comedic value, and no one has a clue that he actually wrote decent test plans.

Rule #5: Do Right by Those Who Work for You and with You

If you're a manager, the previous rules apply to you in triplicate. You're not allowed to fall prey to the dreaded short timer's disease because you are acting like a leader and you are representing the company until the moment you are out the door. If this doesn't make sense to you, then it's likely you weren't supposed to be a manager in the first place.

My move here is an expensive one. I provide a written review to all my direct reports in my last two weeks. Doesn't matter where we are in the review cycle, I take the time to give everyone who works for me a temperature check. Yes, well-written reviews are painful and time-consuming, and yes, I get short timer's syndrome like everyone else, but this small gesture is the best way to explain what these coworkers mean to you.

Rule #6: Don't Volunteer to Do Work After You Leave (or, if You Do, Make Sure You Get a Lot of Money for It)

This is a variant of the guilty conscience problem. This is the result of you sitting on your couch two weeks before you resign, tapping your pencil on your teeth, and exploring the hypothetical look on your boss's face when he realizes his go-to person is leaving.

You like him. You're responsible. You don't want to leave anyone in the lurch. Yes, of course, you can finish those last three projects in your spare time.

Stop.

There are some very good reasons to continue to help out at your past job and, if you choose to do so, I highly recommend gouging your prior employer because this extracurricular work is coming at the worst time possible—when you're starting a new job. The first few weeks of a job are precious. They present the primal lessons of your new career and you only get to hear them once. And what are you doing? Spending your evenings on work from a prior life when what you should be doing is digesting the lessons of the new job.

You will always regret signing up for work to do after you leave.

Rule #7: Don't Give Too Much Notice

Our last variant of guilty conscience. More tapping of the teeth, fretting about how to support this team that you're leaving. Maybe if you give them more time to adjust to a post-you world, it will be easier on everyone.

Again, wrong.

The basic fact is this: you've chosen to leave and you're going to leave. Giving an excessive amount of notice is professional cruel and unusual punishment both for you and for your team because it extends the organization's stress regarding your departure while also preventing your team from doing something critical: moving on.

Your concern is regarding the gap that is created by your absence. This will be your team's concern as well, but a concern is not a solution. As long as you are sitting there busily being present, your team doesn't believe that you are leaving. They're not going to react to your absence until, come Monday morning, they walk by your empty office and feel your absence. Shit, he's gone.

They Know

I got in early on my final Friday at Borland. I'd convinced myself a 5 a.m. start time would create a dramatic last-ditch effort on my committed work. By the time my going-away lunch arrived, I'd successfully booted my computer, stared at the screen for an hour, and packed my boxes.

As 5 p.m. rolled around, I shut down my computer and dragged my feet into my boss's office. "Yeah, so, I didn't finish much of the import/export work."

His comment: "Yeah, no one thought you could do it."

12

Saying No

Somewhere in your third year of being a manager, the management pixies will appear in your office in a puff of sweet-smelling black smoke. There will be three of them, and one will be carrying a gorgeous black top hat.

"Are you LeRoy McManager?"

"I am."

The pixies laugh. "Congratulations, you have passed successfully through three years of management and we're here to reward you. But first, one question: Have you seen *Spider-Man*?"

"The first one or the sequel?"

"The first one."

"I have."

The pixies laugh again. "What do you think is the primary theme in *Spider-Man*, LeRoy McManager?"

"Um, hmmmm . . . Life's a bitch?"

Strangely, the pixies don't laugh. "No, try again. It's important."

"OK, well. Hmmmm . . . Peter's uncle said something they kept yammering about . . . *Oh, I know* . . . With great power comes great responsibility."

The pixies cheer and the one carrying the top hat flutters over to you and drops it in your lap. It's soft and strangely warm. The hat-bearing pixie looks up at you and grins, "You wear this hat when you want people to know who you are."

"And who am I?" You look down at the hat and notice massive white block letters on the front. They read:

I'M THE BOSS.

A slow grin stretches across your face, and you realize the hat has the vague smell of your mom's fresh baked bread. That smell has always given you a strange sense of confidence and you know that whenever you wear that hat, you'll be infused with that sense of confidence.

All three pixies leap into the air, giggling. "Good luck, LeRoy McManager, use your hat well!" More laughing. Another puff of black smoke and they're gone.

You lift the hat slowly in front of your face, staring at the white block letters, soaking in the sense of power the hat gives you, and you put it on.

You stride out of your office, never once wondering why the pixies were giggling so much because, well, you're the boss. The first person sees you walk by in your cloud of confidence, and once you walk around the corner, you don't hear them snicker because, again, you're the boss.

They're laughing because while they know you're the boss, they can see the other side of the hat and it reads:

. . . FOR NOW.

Managers Lose It

I mean it. There are managers out there who are absolutely punch drunk with power, and if you're working for one of these folks, I'm really sorry. You're a resident of Crazy Town, and that means you never know what random crap is going to happen next, and that sucks.

Managers don't start crazy. It's a learned trait, and this chapter explores the single best tactic you can take with both your manager and yourself to avoid trips to Crazy Town. Let's tackle it first with a story about your manager.

You're merrily typing away at your keyboard, hard at work at the next great product, when your boss walks in and says, "Hey, can you work on a Gizzy Flibbet project?"

"Uh, aren't we supposed to be finishing Flubjam? We've barely even started it. It's going to take awhile."

"Oh yes yes, we're still doing Flubjam, but I need you to prototype the Gizzy Flibbet and I need it in two days for a meeting with the execs."

"Ooooooooo-K, you're the boss."

"That's right, I am the boss."

Two days pass and your team briefly pours its soul into the prototype project. Like all investigations, you discover each step of discovery takes three times as long as expected. The final prototype conveys the idea, but the process to create that result has left your team drained and pretty sure finishing the remaining work is going to take a really long time.

When your boss walks into your office, you summarize, "Here it is. It looks good, it'll take awhile and we're now very behind on our Flubjam work. Can we please get back to it?"

Squinting her eyes, she runs her fingertips along the front rim of her top hat. She nods and stares, "OK, *this is great*. Let's do this *and* Flubjam, *and* let's hit the same schedule! Go us!" She turns and leaves the room, leaving your office with the faint smell of bread.

I'll recap. Your boss has just picked the one scenario that involves the most work and has the least chance of succeeding. You're screwed, and while you might think your boss has lost it, you are a coconspirator in this disaster because you didn't do one simple thing: you didn't *say no*.

Losing It

Managers don't lose it simply because the pixies showed up with the top hat, they lose it because those they work with forget to look at the back of the hat. Remember:

Front: I'M THE BOSS.

Back: . . . FOR NOW.

Management is a myth, just like the top hat. We, as employees, believe it's there, so we treat these management types differently. We operate under the assumption that they are the ones who can make decisions. When the team is stuck on a hard problem, we gather in our manager's office, present our case, and then the manager nods and says, "Go that way!" More often than not, we're so happy to be past the hard problem, we don't even question whether it's the right decision or not. "He's got the top hat, so he must be right!"

No no no no. Also? No.

Managers lose it when they are no longer questioned in their decisions. When the team stops questioning authority, the manager slowly starts to believe that his decisions are always good, and while it feels great to be right all the time, it's statistically impossible. The most experienced managers in the world make horribly bad decisions all the time. The good ones have learned how to recover from their decisions with dignity, but more importantly, with help from the team.

Saying no forces an idea to defend itself with facts. It forces a manager under the influence of his top hat to stop and think. Yes, I know that top hat can be intimidating, and yeah, he's the guy who signs the checks, but each time you allow your manager to charge forward with unchecked blind enthusiasm, you only reinforce his perception that he's never wrong. That's a ticket straight to Crazy Town.

Recovering It

My team had just been clobbered by the executive team in the boardroom. We'd been flying high on the sales of the current product and thinking that we could do no wrong, so our presentation for the next version of the product was half-baked. We'd assumed that since the current version was doing so well the executives would ignore our hand-waving about the future, but they didn't.

The Q&A had started pleasantly, but three questions in, when it was clear we were making it up as we were going and there wasn't some master plan behind the flimsy presentation, they started firing the big guns. There is only one extraction technique from these types of beat-downs—you say, "Well, it looks like we need to schedule a follow-up meeting."

The team went into fire drill mode. We needed a product roadmap, we needed it in a week, and we need to rebuild the executive staff's confidence in the team. When the brainstorming began, everyone was rattled. We'd moved from the chosen team to the team who couldn't nail a roadmap presentation. Being shaken, the ideas bouncing around the room were timid. They were designed to appease the folks who had just yelled at us, and while my confidence was shaky, I knew it was time to say no again.

"No, we're not going for mediocre. No, no one wants us to do me-too design. And, no, we're not done with this roadmap until it's something that inspires everyone in the room."

Now, the difference between me standing up in my office and giving a speech on inspirational product roadmaps and a manager who's flirting with Crazy Town because of an executive beat-down is slim, but therein lies the art. Saying no is saying "stop," and in a valley full of people who thrive on endless movement, the ability to strategically choose when it's time to stop is the sign of a manager willing to defy convention.

Never Trust a Pixie

The top hat is not what it seems. Yes, the black velvety elegance is intended to give you confidence, but remember—on the back of that hat is a threat. It's not on the back because the pixies couldn't fit the entire message on the front. It's on the back because they don't want you to live in Crazy Town, but they also don't want you to be paralyzed by the reality that you're potentially one big, bad decision away from being out of a job. They want you to embrace the confidence that the top hat imparts because it will help you make great decisions for yourself, your team, and your product. Some of those great decisions will be the result of blind luck, and some will be because you know what you're doing. However, you will also make some bad decisions, which you will weather sometimes because they weren't that bad, and sometimes purely on your top hat moxie.

And then you're going to make a big, bad decision and you'll remember: "With great power comes great responsibility." As a manager, you are responsible for making great decisions and the best way to do that is to involve as much of the team as possible in every decision.

Your team is collectively smarter than you simply because there are more of them. More importantly, by including them in the decision process and creating a team where they feel they can say no, you're creating trust.

A team that trusts you is going to look out for you. They'll never sit back and watch as you merrily traipse into Crazy Town staring at the back of your hat thinking, "I wonder who gets the top hat next?"

THE PROCESS IS THE PRODUCT

People screw up. Every single one of us. There are the anony-mous screw-ups that no one but us recognizes, and then there are the public ones; the embarrassing disasters where you look up and all eyes on the team are on you. Whoops.

To prevent these screw-ups, the more organized members of the team create process. Their goal is to provide structure around the work we do and to eliminate guessing. These peo-ple are well intentioned, but they still annoy the folks who know, first, we're always going to screw up no matter how much process we have and, second, that screwing up often reveals more useful information than not screwing up.

Process creates a delectable, healthy tension between those who measure and those who create. In this tension, there are useless meetings, yelling in the hallways, and flame mails. I'd like to think the following chapters will help avoid these conflicts, but you need them. Like a good screw-up, a healthy argument provides a different perspective, which, if everyone is paying attention, will help the process evolve, and love it or hate it, the process is how you build a product.

1.0

Max was a mess. We were on our third mojito at the Basin in Saratoga when it just came pouring out of him. The last 72 hours involved this:

- Two days in Los Angeles babysitting a customer's data center

- Four hours of sleep

- Two huge arguments with his wife on the cell phone

- A marathon conference call with his boss, which resulted in a new trip to Chicago in two days

The mojitos might've been talking, but it sounded like Max was sure that his wife was going to leave him; his company was about to crumble; and he was 12 hours and one plane flight from a nervous breakdown.

He said, "Shipping a 1.0 product isn't going to kill you, but it will try."

Understanding 1.0

In your career as a software developer, you're going to be screwed at some point. My advice is keep thinking, don't yell, treat those you work with decently, and you'll be fine. It's valuable experience, but it's nothing compared to 1.0.

1.0 is developing the first version of a new product. It's what all those start-ups are busily doing right now. They're working on some 1.0 idea that's good enough that a handful of bright people will forgo their lives in support of the chance of being right. *See*, we had a great idea. We're bazillionaires and we were right.

Most of those startups fail.

Before Fucked Company, failing was a quiet, somber thing. The dot-com explosion made colossal flameouts front-page news, and everyone discovered what most of us already knew.

Really. Most startups fail.

Why?

To understand the difficulty of 1.0, I need to give you a model for understanding how a 1.0 software product actually shows up. I've designed just such a model by heavily borrowing from a theory known as Maslow's Hierarchy of Needs, which is worth talking about all by its lonesome.

Maslow's theory contends that as humans meet their basic needs, they seek to satisfy successively higher needs that occupy a set hierarchy, as shown in Figure 13-1.

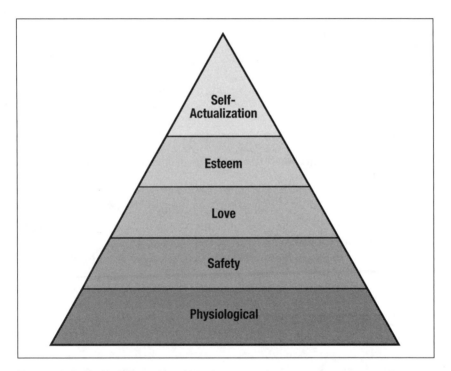

Figure 13-1 Maslow's Hierarchy of Needs

At the bottom of the pyramid is the biggest area of need: physiological needs. These are the basics: food, drink, air, sleep, etc. The idea is that you won't be able to focus on anything else in the hierarchy if these needs aren't met. Think of it like this: who cares about falling in love if you can't breathe?

Moving up the hierarchy, you have safety needs, love/belonging, esteem, and finally, the oddly named "self-actualization" tip of the pyramid, which is our instinctual need to make the most of our unique abilities. Translation: Writers write, singers sing.

There's a fine entry in Wikipedia regarding Maslow's hierarchy if I've piqued your interest (see `http://en.wikipedia.org/wiki/Maslow's_hierarchy_of_needs`). Personally, as a manager of humans, I stare at the hierarchy when dealing with folks on the edge. The hierarchy gives me insight into where exactly a person is stressing out. Are they in need of career advice? (Easy.) Or do they need marriage advice? (Harder.)

Rands 1.0 Hierarchy

In thinking about the difficulties of 1.0, I realized that Maslow's model applied to shipping the first version of a product. There's a hierarchy that defines what you need to build in order to ship 1.0, and it looks like Figure 13-2.

Sidebar regarding charts and graphs: Phillippe Kahn, the founder of Borland, told a great story about statistics that I think equally applies to charts and graphs. The story is, "Did you know it's a statistical fact that people with larger feet tend to be better spellers? [Insert awe.] It's because people with bigger feet are older."

Charts 'n' graphs paint the world in a clean, linear fashion that serves one purpose: supporting the message of the author. Do not trust charts 'n' graphs, but don't let that lack of trust blind you to the intent of the story.

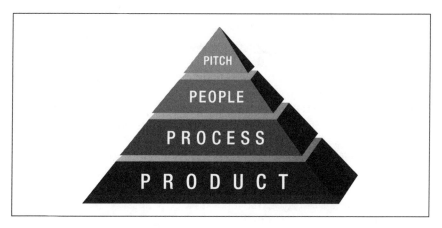

Figure 13-2 Rands 1.0 Hierarchy

Pitch

At the top of the hierarchy, there's Your Great Idea. I'm calling it "pitch" because I've got this alliteration thing going on. You can't get anywhere in building a product or a company without a phenomenal pitch. It doesn't matter if you're Mr. Charisma; you've got to have the idea because it defines the structure and constraints of everything below it. If you don't have the idea, you don't know who to hire, which is the second layer—people.

Before we talk about this second layer, let me first congratulate you. I'm tripping over myself happy that you've discovered the Next Big Thing, but there are some basic facts to pay attention to. The first is:

Fact #1: You're in a hurry.

You're a fool if you think you have exclusive rights to your pitch. There are too many bright people staring at exactly the same infinite pile of evolving information to assume your innovation is original. The only thing that gives you this right is delivering 1.0, and first, you're going to need some people.

People

With your pitch in hand, you're going to find the people to build your idea. These are your founders. These are the folks who will not only build your 1.0, but more importantly, your engineering culture. Their arrival presents a challenge and a twist to the pyramid.

Your first few hires walk into a blank slate. Yes, they're believers in the pitch—otherwise they wouldn't be in the building—but now it's their pitch, which means they're going to ask the hard questions because they've got some skin in the game. These hard questions are going to help them start making decisions about the eventual products.

As the keeper of the pitch, you're going to try to stay involved, but you simply can't be there for every decision. Your job is to listen and watch incessantly so that you can detect how the decisions and actions of your people are slowly changing your pitch. This leads us to our twist. The Rands 1.0 Hierarchy is much scarier than Maslow's, because it looks like Figure 13-3.

There's a good reason why folks don't build their pyramids like this—they fall over. The only way to keep them from falling over is to constantly push one side or the other. This is your startup. This impractical concept with your pitch sitting at the bottom defining everything above it. What will kill you about 1.0 will be how much time you're going to spend trying to keep this pyramid balanced, which brings us back to the topic at hand: people.

Fact #2: No one is indispensable.

Now, I'm a people person. This entire book is devoted to figuring out how to make sure folks get along and get stuff done, but we're not talking about an established company here, we're talking about 1.0 and the rules are different because you are an unknown quantity and everyone is expecting you to fail.

Figure 13-3 Rands 1.0 Hierarchy

Ever built a fire? What do you need? A match, some paper, and some kindling wood that catches fire easily. Your first three hires are your kindling. Their job is not to define the product roadmap, their job is to get things moving, and if things aren't moving, you need to get some more wood.

At my startup, I was brought in as the first engineering manager. The founders had brought on two free electrons with totally different temperaments (see Chapter 30 for more on free electrons). One was burning the midnight oil on getting a working prototype done. He was fully aware we'd throw the whole thing away, but he knew that the ability to see the idea in code would change everyone's opinion of what we were doing. It would make the pitch real.

The other electron also loved the pitch, but he was working on infrastructure for future products. *He was what?* Yes, we had no product and one of our key hires was already investing in the future. When is investing in the future a bad idea? How about when the now is not defined? The free electron was working under the assumption that 1.0 would be successful, and while I appreciated his enthusiasm, let's remember fact #0: startups almost always fail.

I spent some time with the free electron and, as it often goes with very bright people on a mission, it was clear he wasn't going to be swayed, so I let him go. That day. One quick meeting with our VP and it was done.

As you'll learn in Chapter 30 (on free electrons), you don't run into these types of stunning engineers often. Firing a free electron is pretty stupid for most companies because they have so much potential, but here's the deal: you aren't a company until 1.0 is done. A great way to topple your fledging pyramid is to hire folks who are not getting the product done with a sense of urgency. Get 1.0 done and then worry what's next.

Process

There is no word that irks engineers more than *process*. Try it right now. Get everyone in your office and say something like, "I've defined a new process to assist our bug triage." Watch their faces sag. They hear "busywork." They think "management is trying to justify itself."

This is not the word that defines the third level of the hierarchy.

Fact #3: Process defines communication.

Process is the means by which your team communicates. Whether this is via a wiki, e-mail, or the hallway, any team larger than one needs to define a means to share information. This is not an argument for specifications, documentation, or a whiteboard filled with dos and don'ts. You just need to agree how you're going to share information.

When your second engineer decides, "Yes, I'm going to capture my design decisions in a wiki," that's process. When your third engineer starts tracking bugs on that huge whiteboard in the meeting room, that's process. It doesn't have to be good, it doesn't even have to be universally agreed upon on, it just has to be stuck in a place where everyone can see it.

SourceSafe was the repository of choice when I landed at my first startup. Stop laughing. It did a fine job with a team of six engineers who had zero time to worry about source control. Sure, it was slow as hell and lost a day's work here and there because of various hiccups, but we were working on 1.0, and who had time to think about something more reliable?

Roland did.

Roland was a junior engineer and he was a Perforce fan. Roland did what any good employee of a startup would do. Over the course of a weekend, he set up a Perforce server, rewrote all of our build tools, and scheduled a 10 a.m. meeting on the following Monday, promising Krispy Kreme doughnuts. His message: "This is the way it is. Everything works better. Thank you and have a doughnut."

In a weekend, Roland fixed a major flaw in our process (crappy tools) and also demonstrated another fact of the hierarchy.

Fact #4: Each layer shapes and moves those near it.

A sure sign of a healthy pyramid is that one layer invades another. Think of each change to people, process, and pitch as a shove in one direction. This movement requires compensation in the other layers, otherwise the whole thing falls over. Roland's decision to change the engineering process pissed off some folks. We lost some time to some source management edge cases that Roland hadn't thought of, but, within a week, we'd adjusted. Even the most vocal opponent of the change ended up in Roland's office arguing about how we could make it better.

If, in your organization, your pyramid is not constantly adjusting to keep itself upright, something's wrong. If the new folks aren't testing the pitch, they either don't buy it or they don't get it. If your engineers aren't arguing about the way they develop software *all the time*, they're becoming stagnant, and that trickles down to your pitch and trickles up to your product.

A great stagnation warning sign during 1.0 is when someone decides to create an organization chart defining "This is who does what." Now, investors and outside parties need this org chart to get a sense of whether you're real or not, but your 1.0 team does not. The whiteboard in the corner of the room, which lists who is doing what, is your org chart. The definition and hierarchy an org chart portrays is the first step in creating a culture of secrecy in your org. That might work for Apple, but you're not Apple, yet. You're hope and hard work.

Product

At some point, you're going to need to fake being done. You're going to need to release something that barely looks like your pitch because you don't have product until a neutral party stares at something.

Fact #5: You don't have a company until you have a product.

Product is not pitch. Pitch is the three-sentence idea that gave you the credibility to hire the people. The people argued about the pitch, they created process to refine and develop the pitch, and that changed it. The pyramid wobbled hither and fro during all of this. Maybe it fell completely over and you scrambled to stack those layers up again. Good job, there. You still don't have product.

The neutral parties, your customers, need to see what you've been building because all your people are completely insane. All that healthy shifting of the pyramid has been taxing them. Each shove forced them to adjust their perspective of the pitch, their relation to it, and adapting to change is fucking exhausting. Folks who say "I like change" are not currently working at a startup. Folks at a startup don't say much because they're busy adapting to the latest pyramid shift.

This state of constant change is the leading cause of startup burnout, and it's also the reason you've got to get that product out. The perspective of the neutral party is essential validation because you're nuts. Your pitch has been dissected and redefined so many times that it may no longer be something that is useful. A neutral party doesn't care about the pitch, your people, or any of the pyramid shoving you've been up to; they just care whether the product is useful.

Using the Pyramid

At no point will you ever draw this hierarchy on a whiteboard during an organizational crisis and say, "*Folks, pay attention to the pyramid—so says the Rands.*" The idea is to give you a tool that reminds you, "Hey, it's all connected!" The pitch guides the people. The people refine the pitch. People and pitch create process and product, and, yeah, it's all a big mess and that's why startups fail.

The pyramid gives you a hazy map to think about the problems your company might face. People will yell in the hallway and it might sound like they're arguing about product, but keep listening, maybe it's process. Even worse (better?), maybe it's pitch. Your one job as keeper of the pitch is figuring out which layer of the pyramid is being tested, and then figure out which way to shove the pyramid. This leads us to our last fact:

Fact #6: The lower the failure, the higher the cost.

A year into my startup, the founders were at a crossroads. We were doing an enterprise web application that was built for onsite deployment. Problem was, everyone was going loopy about hosted services. The pitch there was: "Look how much time and energy I'll save you by hosting this application in my data center, not yours." This idea flew in the face of years of Oracle, PeopleSoft, and IBM domination of that huge pile of business software and hardware sitting in your data center, but it was the Internet and the Internet was going to save the world.

The founders changed their pitch. "We'll just create copies of the software in our data center! We'll save money keeping our bits close to home!" No huge difference there? Wrong. This adjustment to our pitch changed the fundamental architecture of our product. Rather than have hundreds of customized versions of our software sitting in various data centers, we had to have one copy of our software that was configurable to each of our customers' needs, and that wasn't the product we designed.

It wasn't an instant disaster. We had piles of money to throw at this transformation, but the transition cost became so great that we stopped working on anything except getting the hosted application working and, right about then, the bubble burst.

Let's call failure a really bad decision. It's when you choose to change something and that change percolates up through the pyramid. If you make a bad decision regarding version control, well, you can probably adjust to that. You can fire a free electron and probably find another bright person who can channel the pitch better, but you're probably going to rattle more than you think. A failure of pitch is a structural failure that affects your entire company. Everything in your company depends on the vision that you've presented and screwing that up can be fatal.

Building Culture

If you've actually got a pitch ready to go, again, that's terrific. This totally conceptual model I've thrown together doesn't cover some major topics that you need to understand. How are you going to fund this thing? Where do you find VCs? Where do you find great people? Your life will become an endless list of questions and decisions and you'll probably forget everything I just wrote in your frenetic sprint to keep your pitch alive, so I'll simplify. The hierarchy I describe is not a model for how to build a great product; it's a picture that describes the construction of the culture of your company. That's what you're really building in 1.0. A lasting, interesting culture that, if you're lucky, continues to produce great products.

Think of your five favorite companies and think about what made them successful. Yes, they probably had a great 1.0. Think about when you first saw a Mac. Think of the first time you saw Netscape. How about your first useful search on Google? Those products are the end result of people killing themselves to get the damned thing out the door, but these people weren't just creating that product. Their work defined the culture of the company, and that is what modeled their future success.

Taking Time to Think

Lunch at Don Giovanni's with Phillip. He's amped. We haven't even seen our waiter and he's already cleared the table and is scribbling furiously on the white paper tablecloth.

"See, we needed to speed up our release cycle, which is, of course, insane, but we figured out a way! We call it train releases. We've got four releases going at the same time and a train leaves the station every month. If a feature is ready to go, it gets on the train, and if it's not, it waits for the next train. We've already released two trains in six weeks!"

I nod, watching the scribbles become increasingly incoherent. I'd buy Phillip a nice glass of Chianti to take the edge off, but he's a Mormon, so I try the truth.

"Phil, you're screwed twice. First, you're screwed because you're going to need, at least, twice the staff to qualify these ever-increasing releases, and you're a startup. You've got one QA guy, and if he hasn't blown a fuse yet, just wait a month. Second, and most important, you've got no downtime. You've got no time to design because everyone is going to be panicked about which train they're supposed to be riding.

"Phil, in order to create, you've got to think."

Reacting vs. Thinking

Why can't you think when you're busy?

Dumb question, right? Answer: "I can't think because I'm busy."

Wrong. You can't think because when you're busy, you're not thinking, you're reacting.

Example: You walk into my office and start yelling, "Rands, it's two days from shipping and we've just found a bad bug, a showstopper. What do we do? Are we screwed?"

I will respond and my response might look like thinking, but I'm not doing anything creative because I've dealt with the showstopper two days before ship scenario *in every product I've ever built*. Survived it each time, too. Got some great stories. It's that experience I'm using when you walk into my office and tell me the sky is falling. I'm not actually doing anything new, I'm just telling you the story of how I propped the sky up last time.

Yes, you can argue that one can be exquisitely creative when one's hair is on fire. It's the necessity is the mother of invention argument; but, seriously, if your hair's on fire, are you going to take the time to seriously consider all hair-dousing techniques, or are you just going to stick your head in the nearest convenient bucket before it really hurts? Panic is the mother of the path of least resistance.

You won't be a successful manager without well-developed react instincts. A quiver full of experience gives you all sorts of arrows to shoot at problems, and the timing and accuracy of some of those shots will be brilliant, but your quiver will slowly empty unless you take the time to think.

For the sake of this article, let's partition your brain—one half is the creative brain. This is the part of your brain that is the source of inspiration. The other half of your brain is your reactive brain. This is the part of the brain that loves it when the sky is falling because it gets to move so gosh darned quick.

Your react brain doesn't actually like to think because thinking is messy. Thinking involves slowing down and actually soaking in a problem, and your react brain thrives in the familiar. Your creative brain loves the unknown. It's a sponge and it's only happy when it's full of new ideas. This is part of the reason thinking is hard to pull off at work—it doesn't fit nicely into the daily course of business because it's full of mind-bending paradoxes and uncomfortable realities your mechanical manager is going to barf all over. Some examples:

- Thinking is not something you can constrain by time or a meeting. There is no beginning and there is no end—you never know when you're done.

- Doing more thinking always pays off, but time is money and you've got 27 other meetings this week.

- The more people you include in the thinking process, the more genuine ideas you'll find, but the process of finding those ideas will linearly slow down with each person who shows up.

- Everyone thinks differently.

The time to kick off your deep thinking is right after your last major release. It's when every single lesson of the prior release is forefront in the team's mind. They've just gone through the crunch where they had to stare at each poor design decision illuminated by repeated painful deferral of bugs. They're exhausted, but they have hope because they know they can fix it in the next release.

Getting Started

The first step is defining a time when the team can think. In the past, I was a fan of kicking things off with an offsite. A good solid day of thinking somewhere other than corporate headquarters where folks can forget about their daily professional woes. The problem with this is that while everyone loves a field trip, the day is an illusion. Sure, the coffee tastes different and, yeah, everyone seems really excited about the next version, but tomorrow you're going back to headquarters, which is where you're going to do 95 percent of your actual thinking. You've got to create a thinking-conducive environment in your natural setting.

Start with two meetings a week. The first is a brainstorm meeting and the second is a prototype meeting. Both are, at least, an hour long.

Make sure there is time between the brainstorm and prototype meeting. Give everyone involved time to stew on the results of the brainstorm meeting. Conversely, you don't want to wait too long to see a prototype because you'll forget the context of the initial brainstorm. Once-a-week meetings are a study in futility because folks forget everything during the course of a weekend and meetings end up rehashing the same thoughts from the week before.

Players

When the meetings begin, you need a driver. Maybe it's you, maybe it's not. There's another paradox here. Structured thinking kills thinking, but unstructured thinking leads to useless chaos. Your meeting driver must be able to swerve the conversation back and forth between the two extremes, but generally keep it in the middle. Organics (see Chapter 28 for more on organics) tend to be best at this. More on this in a bit when we figure out if your meeting is actually working.

Whom to invite? This is the hard one. If you invite every single person on the team, you'll get nothing done . . . even with the world's best driver. You've got to start small and let the momentum build. This is where you might initially piss people off because everyone wants to sit in this meeting because everyone has an opinion. If you have an idea of what the initial topics will be, invite those you know have an educated opinion. If you have no clue where to start with topics, roll the dice . . . pick at random. You never know what you're going to find in the minds of engineers. The good news is that one of the best signs of a productive design process is that the players change. More on this in a moment.

One land mine you've got to be aware of in your attendee selection is obstructionists. These are folks who've fallen into a total react lifestyle. You can easily identify them by their tendency to map every new idea against previous experience and then declare the idea "unoriginal." The reasons for this attitude varies. Maybe they were early designers of the product and can't escape from the original design. Maybe it's the fear of the unknown. Whatever the cause, these folks are a creativity buzz kill and are not folks you want to invite to your initial brainstorm meetings.

Content

The goal for the first brainstorm meeting is to start reliving the pain of the last release. What bug did you hate to defer? What feature didn't get pulled off? Who hates this UI? Everyone? Yeah, I thought so. Hey, who is our customer anyway? You want to walk out of your first brainstorm meeting with five hot topics that folks want to address.

The second meeting is your prototype meeting. You want to see the results of the last brainstorm meeting in a prototype . . . paper . . . code . . . wireframe . . . bulleted list. It doesn't matter as long as there is documented evidence of what occurred in the prior meeting. Maybe you just had a list of customer types? How about a list of the five things the team hates about the product? Your goal here is documented continuity between meetings. This documentation will eventually turn into mock-ups or actual working prototypes, but out of the gate, keep the documentation focused on remembering what the hell happened last time.

When you do get to mock-ups or prototypes, keep them lightweight and devoid of detail. If it's week three and the team is arguing about which icons fit where, you're too deep. I'm a fan of wireframes when it comes to visually wiring an application together. They give all the geometry of a visual idea without suggesting a look or feel.

Is It Working?

OK, you're two weeks into the Rands Creativity Plan and it's going poorly. No one said anything during the first meeting because they've never been asked their opinion before. The meeting consisted of you in front of the whiteboard and a lot of nodding. This lack of brainstorming content led to a very dull prototype meeting, so you stuck with more brainstorming. Week two rolled around and folks started talking except, well, they were yelling because there's a fundamental disagreement about who the customer actually is. That's painful progress except when you roll into your second prototype meeting and everyone's silent again because who wants to be yelled at?

Good work. Really.

It's a big deal to mentally stumble about and bump into shit during your initial brainstorm meetings. This seeming lack of mental coordination is what finding innovation is all about . . . but you still need to understand if you're making progress. Some things you can look for as the weeks pass:

- **Are decisions being made?** Is the group working well enough to make a decision? Yes? Good.

- **Are decisions being revisited?** Is the group limber enough to go backward to refine a previous decision? Even better.

- **Are decisions constantly being revisited?** OK, problem here. Your team has spun into creative nirvana. A good time to step back and apply a little structure to the process. Reviewing decisions to date is a good way to find structure and move forward. Oh, you weren't writing down the results of brainstorm meetings? Oops. Start now.

- **Are the players changing?** If you're four weeks in and the faces at the table haven't changed, you might have a problem. If you're working on a sizable project, there is no way you picked the right brainstorm team from the onset. The diversity of thought sitting outside of the room must be brought into the conversation. Time to start mixing it up.

- **Are basic truths about your design showing up?** These are the gems of brainstorm. These are decisions that are made that define the basic design of your problem. You'll know these when they show up, stand up to scrutiny, and eventually start virally wandering the hallways.

- **Is it therapy or work?** If you've just been through a brutal release, the team is going to spend the first brainstorming meetings venting. That's OK, they need it. If it's week three and you're still on the vent, it's time to make changes.

- **Are holy shit moments occurring?** Similar to the basic truth discovery, but louder and infrequent. *"Holy shit*, we're completely wrong." Holy shits are disruptive, but are a good sign of a limber creative process.

- **Is the to-do list growing or shrinking?** If you're early on in the design phase, it should be growing. If you're getting close to the end of your design phase, it better be getting smaller. I know engineers want to solve every problem in the product in any given major release, but *that never ever happens ever*. Better is the enemy of done, and if it's your project, you need to draw a line on what topics/ideas you intend to tackle and stick to it.

My rule of thumb is if you aren't staring at one hard decision per meeting . . . you might be wasting your time. You've got the wrong people and/or the wrong driver and while it sure is fun to have an hour to chat . . . that's all you're doing. Chatting.

When to Stop

If your meetings are healthy, the meetings will naturally move from one topic to another. Decisions are built, ideas are vetted, yelling occurs, and prototypes are reviewed. I've found that these meetings will slowly die off as you move from hardcore design into serious development. If they don't, then you're probably becoming addicted to thinking, and while that sounds appealing, you're not working for a university, you're working for your shareholders and they want to see new product yesterday. You can still fine-tune design during the depths of development, but the trend you want to see in your meetings is that questions are being answered, not created.

Fighting Stagnation

Google knows you've got to take time to think. It is rumored they ask their employees to spend one day a week working on their own projects. Do that math. Google is investing 20 percent of the engineering budget on thinking. I'm sure that nothing comes from a majority of those projects, but Google gets two wins out of the program. First, some of the projects create value for the company. It's probably one in five, but that's not the real value. Google is creating a culture of thinking by allowing their employees to wander about and bump into shit.

I don't know what you do and I don't know what you build. I am certain that if you don't demonstrate creative thinking in what you build, you're screwed because you, your team, and your product will stagnate. Kicking off brainstorming meetings are a tricky proposition. They are poorly defined, hard to run, and harder to measure. What comes out of these meetings might be brilliance or stupidity . . . The difference between the two is magnificently slim. Good luck.

The Soak

In 2006, I gave a presentation at South by Southwest. My pitch was this: in creating a startup, you're going to be faced with a thousand seemingly inconsequential decisions. Tucked among those thousands of decisions are five decisions that actually matter. These decisions will change the face of your company. What I didn't say was that I believe it's next to impossible to figure out which decisions matter and which ones do not.

How depressing.

Here's the deal: you can spend a lot of energy deciding what the big decisions might be, but that's much less important than making the decision . . . educated guess or gut instinct. There's a pile of thoughts on creating decision-friendly environments in Chapter 14, but that chapter focuses on the idea of thinking in a team scenario, and I want to talk about when you choose to take your thinking solo.

Let's start with the most infuriating e-mail you've ever received. I'm not talking about that jerk in tech support who is simply stupid, I'm talking about the e-mail from someone you trust . . . a peer . . . pissing you off in e-mail. You're going to want to react to this e-mail in the same manner as if I came into your office and punched you in the face. It's your animal brain at work and it served you well when you were living in a cave doing the hunter-gathering thing because reacting slowly meant you were eaten or punched again.

Now. You have time to soak.

The soak is when you plant the seed of a thought in your brain and let it bump around in a rich stew of ideas, facts, and whatever other random crap that seems to relate. The soak is a protected activity that will rarely occur during your busy day because you're busy reacting to the familiar never-ending flood of things to do. The goal of the soak is simple: an original thought. Whatever the problem is that you're stewing on, you want to find a glimmer of inspiration that transforms your response from a predictable emotional flame-o-gram into a strategic considered thought.

Emotion and Ignorance

At a prior gig, I was finally hitting my stride. After a two-year awkward getting-to-know-the-company phase, I was in the groove. I knew who was doing what, who was hungry, and who was coasting. I'd turned a small bright idea of a product into a successful moneymaker, so my boss decided to saddle me with something completely different. An entirely new product built on technology I'd never used. It was a strategic-shift product for the company, which meant everyone would be watching. This visibility would amplify potential fuck-ups. This was the career-defining product for me.

Holy shit.

Having no clue where to start a new project and wanting to rip someone apart in e-mail share one important characteristic. The best move in both cases is to start with a good long soak.

I break soaking activities into two buckets: *active soaks* and *passive soaks*. The active soaks are activities that you can direct and usually involve gathering content, whereas passive soaks are activities when you just point your brain in a random direction and pray. Passive soaks are where the real work gets done. Let's start with the first.

Active Soaking

Ask dumb questions. Your first job when faced with ignorance is information acquisition, and, hopefully, there are folks out there who've already done some soaking. These folks have some facts, ideas, and opinions regarding whatever the problem might be, and you need to hear them all. The first five of these conversations can be awkward for managers because it'll be obvious after your first two questions ("What is it?" and "How does it work?") that you have absolutely no clue what's going on and you think it's a manager's job to appear clueful.

Wrong. It's a manager's job to be clued in. You work in an industry popu-lated with engineers, and these are folks who are paid a lot of money to care about the details, and that means they see right past feigned knowledge. Sure, they're not saying anything because you're the boss, but, um, you look stupid.

Soaking starts out uncomfortable, but with each ignorant question you ask, you're adding content to that managerial brain of yours. Asking dumb ques-tions is the best way to start figuring out what is actually going on. Furthermore, asking any question of your team is a handy way to indirectly say, "I care about what we're doing enough to ask you what you think."

Pitch a stranger. Once you've asked enough dumb questions, a picture will start to form in your mind about what exactly you're doing. It's not a complete picture, it's more a rough sketch coupled with the mild relief that accompanies the sudden absence of ignorance. Now you've got to test your understanding with a qualified someone who is willing to listen to you ramble. Pitch this person on your picture and see what happens. Lots of nodding? Great, it's coming together. Blank stare? Oops, time for more dumb questions starting with the person you just pitched.

What I find when I pitch a stranger is that the words coming out of my mouth have very little to do with the picture that's in my head. The act of linearly mapping my thoughts into words and sentences exposes flaws or gaps in my thinking that I never find when the ideas are swirling around my head. This leads me to our next step.

Write it down, throw it away, write it down again. Once your stranger is no longer totally confused by your idea, it's time to write it down. This is the same process as pitching the stranger in that you're finding another medium to test your idea. The stranger gave you a chance to verbalize your pitch; writing it down routes your idea through a completely different part of your brain and then down through your fingers. Seeing the words on a piece of paper or flat panel monitor will, once again, expose gaps you can't see in the picture in your mind. Those gaps prove you've got more dumb questions, so go ask them, write it down again, and then throw it away. That's right, don't just close the document window; you need to get rid of everything you just wrote down. Toss it, empty the trash, and step away from the computer.

I know you're attached to some part of that document that you wrote—some witty thought that elegantly captured an angle on your problem—but remember what we're trying to solve here. This isn't whether or not you should get a blueberry-orange muffin on the way to work, this is a decision that matters, and solving it elegantly means you want to visit and revisit your response as many times as possible. Consigning your first written draft to the ether might forever lose a piece of wit, but if that wit shows up in the second draft, I guarantee that it belongs there and you'll never lose it again.

Passive Soaking

Once you've done all your active content acquisition, once you've pitched some strangers, once you've written it down a few times, you need to stop actively working on the problem. Remove that sticky from your screen, hide those second drafts on your desktop, and just stop working on it. Yes, you need to make a decision, you need to respond to whatever the problem is, and while I am saying you should remove all the physical artifacts of your active soak, you're not going to stop. You can't. Your brain won't let you.

Back to the original flame mail from your friend. You've received these before and you know the absolute wrong thing to do is immediately respond. Of course, your animal brain is dying to do so because *it feels so good to punch back*, but it's never the right move because your animal brain is defending itself, it's not resolving anything other than proving *boy, can I punch back or what*? My advice regarding flame-o-grams and hard decisions is the same. Sleep on it.

A night's rest is one of the best ways to calm and alter your perspective on a problem. Ever gone to bed at night when the sky is falling and awoken to a blissfully simple way to easily prop the sky up? How'd that happen? The answer is, your brain never stops working. Better yet, it has the unique ability to subconsciously construct elegant solutions to hard problems when you least expect it. Call it inspiration, call it intuition, but don't stare at it too long because it's a shy ability. It does it's best work when no one knows it's there.

Soaking Takes Time

Don't tell anyone I work with, but I earn a majority of my pay during the 40-minute drive to work in the morning. I get in the car with my cup of coffee, hit the road, and let my mind wander to whatever music is playing. Never do I think, "OK, Phil flamed me pretty hard yesterday . . . how am I going to deal with this?" My mind stumbles, it strikes out in random directions, and I never know where it'll end up. Still, if I've spent time actively soaking on the Phil problem the day before, my wandering often ends up somewhere Phil-like, and sometimes, the mental journey reveals a nugget of inspiration.

As practical advice goes, the soak is pretty thin. If your boss is waiting for you to weigh in on a critical decision, I am not advising you to say, "I have no clue what to do, I'm going to go ask dumb questions, pitch a stranger, write it down and then throw it away, and then forget everything I did." What I am saying is that any big decision, any big problem, deserves time and consideration. If you've got years of experience under your belt, you can probably wing it pretty well, but you're still going to be faced with situations where the right decision is to not decide, but think.

The soak is, hands down, the favorite part of my job. What I'm doing when I'm soaking on something is an act of creation. It's design work. It's strategy. It's removing the emotion and ignorance from a problem and then constructing an original solution that shows those I work with that I'm actively caring about what I do.

Malcolm Events

The nerd frenzy around the original *Jurassic Park* was significant and led by the promise of lifelike computer animation. This was a win-win for engineers. Not only do we tap into our preadolescent dinosaur love, but we also get to watch the first movie where dinosaurs actually show up, and, by the way, using *the tools we wrote.* OK, so I was at Borland at the time, and we wrote programming languages and applications in the early '90s, but *those ILM guys are just down the street. We're buds.*

Strangely, 13 years later, the memory that has stuck with me from the movie was a quote by Jeff Goldblum's character, Ian Malcolm. He was sitting in the Jurassic SUV, busily hitting on Laura Dern, trying to explain chaos theory to a paleobotanist, when he made a comment that burned itself into my brain.

He was demonstrating chaos theory by placing drops of water on the top of her raised hand and asking, "Which way is it going to fall?" (Smooth, really smooth, Jeff.) The drops fell in a different direction each time, and Malcolm attributed this to "the principle of tiny variations—the orientations of the hairs on your hand, the amount of blood distending in the skin, [they] never repeat, and vastly affect the outcome . . ."

For you nerds out there who want to know more, go read about the butterfly effect. But for me, the quote encapsulates an essential part of practical software design. In the years since the movie, I've mutated the quote into "Seemingly insignificant events that are intent on screwing you in an unlikely way." These events are named after Ian Malcolm, as they are called *Malcolm events.*

We're in a Hurry

We're always in a hurry in the Silicon Valley. If we're not making new stuff, we're making stuff to help us make new stuff. Our stuff-building process varies from company to company, but it usually follows a cycle that looks like this:

Design: Brainstorm new stuff to make. Talk a lot. Throw a lot away. Talk some more.

Development: Less talking, more doing. Engineers are heads-down and managers are wondering what they're supposed to do.

Deployment: More talking, some yelling, managers are busily keeping everyone from killing each other, and then it's suddenly . . . done.

We're in the design phase right now, you and I. I'm the manager, you're the senior engineer, and we're brainstorming our next release. We've each got a fuzzy picture of what we want to do in the next release, but it's not clear. There's nothing that defines the picture, so we're just throwing ideas against the wall to see what's going to stick.

Nothing appears to be sticking until you say something off the cuff; I take the idea, riff on it, write it on the whiteboard and *wham* . . . that's the Feature. It's the piece of work, the design, that will define your release. We know it is because we both sit there staring at the whiteboard at the Feature knowing that this moment will define everything after it. Doesn't happen often, savor it.

This is not a Malcolm event. This moment is akin to a holy shit moment when you first understand a marvelous new technology. You must have these moments to have an inspired release, but you haven't been screwed by a Malcolm event, yet.

Let's keep moving.

Great, so we've got the Feature. Now the frenzy begins. We can't keep our paws off the whiteboard because we know that in the next 15 minutes, the rest of the features are just going to come pouring out. Now, during the frenzy, a whole pile of decisions are going to be made, and while we're valiantly going to try to capture them on our whiteboard, we're going to miss a few.

I want to pick one of these missed decisions. At first glance, it's not a big decision. In fact, in the creative frenzy that is the discovery of a release, it's a really small decision. When the meeting is over, we forget that it was made because we're digesting the mental high imparted by this discovery of the Feature.

Problem is, this decision does matter. What you don't know is that this decision clarifies the Feature in a critical way for those who weren't in the first meeting frenzy. By the way, *that's everyone*.

No one knows this yet, but this is your Malcolm event.

Understanding Malcolm Events

It's a month later, and development has begun and more folks are involved. Someone asks you a question about the Feature and the answer is the decision that was forgotten. No big deal, you answer the question and move on. A week later, you get asked the same question by a QA guy. Haven't you already answered this question? Yeah, you did. OK, no big deal. Here's the answer.

Another month passes and by your count, you've been asked the same clarifying question ten times and you're wondering, "Don't people get it? Isn't it obvious what the answer is?"

No, they don't. They weren't in the religious experience that was your original design meeting and, more bad news, these people who are asking the questions—they aren't the problem. It's the people who aren't asking. It's the ones who are assuming an answer to the question and not asking. They're thinking, "Well, if it was important, someone would've told me or written it down, right?"

A Malcolm event is when a seemingly insignificant event screws up your release in an unlikely way. In the case of this clarifying decision, it's a poor communication tax. Everyone is wondering about this odd aspect of the Feature and in that confusion they are wasting time and they are wasting money.

The release might go swimmingly. The Malcolm event might just be an annoyance where, in every meeting, someone asks *the same lame question*. Or maybe you're not so lucky. Maybe the documentation folks never bother to ask a clarification question and your documentation describes your Feature poorly. Even worse, maybe the developer responsible for the Feature spends a month developing to his version of reality before you install a build and figure out that people can't read your mind.

There's a wide spectrum of cost for Malcolm events, so let's try to avoid them. Here's how.

Artifacts

Someone who has been reading this piece has had their hand up for most of the chapter. OK, what's your question?

"Rands, you're talking about specifications! Functional specifications! Interaction designs, visual designs, and wireframes! Who doesn't love wire—"

OK, hand down.

No, this is not a piece that is going to describe the many benefits of writing stuff down and, yes, there are many benefits, but this is a heavy-handed approach for avoiding Malcolm events.

Remember, we're talking about the little stuff here. I'm not talking about the broad strokes of a release, I'm talking about the seemingly inconsequential details that are intent on screwing you. A well-written specification will document all of your details, but do you have time to write and maintain specifications? I don't. I'm coming up on a decade and a half of working at fairly successful companies, and I can count the number of useful specifications I've read on two hands. Really.

The issue isn't that specifications are a bad idea, it's that they are time-consuming, and remember, we're in a hurry. Still, something does need to be captured because the first thing we need to avoid a Malcolm event is an artifact.

An artifact captures an essential piece of knowledge. Yes, it can be a specification or a blurb or a picture or a priority or even an owner. The key is you've got to know it's essential to capture this artifact because you've been here before and you know that if this piece of knowledge is not well understood across the organization, you're screwed.

I learned this the hard way during the second release of our product at the startup. In an early brainstorming meeting, our VP of sales spent a good hour explaining the need for better performance. We all nodded knowing that a future release of the product would include a new application server that would improve our performance issues. The problem was, no one ever told the VP "no," and worse, when the product shipped, the performance was slightly worse. When the VP found out, he was in my office yelling for a solid 30 minutes.

In our next release, we correctly decided to hold off the application server for another six months, and every single feature list I wrote had the following line, in bold, at the top of the list: "No performance increases in this release."

Malcolm event detection is simply the hardest part of your job because it's the art of identifying the significantly insignificant, and I'd like to provide some great advice here, but my advice is simple and unfortunate. The only way you're going to learn to identify potential Malcolm events is by going through some horrible, horrible experiences.

Sorry.

Binders

Great, so using your past horrible experiences, you've captured an artifact. Let's say it's a semi-scribbled drawing of a brilliant UI design. Congratulations on your foresight to write something down. Now what? Where do you keep that drawing? In your Moleskine? Well, that's fashionable and useless. An artifact stuffed in your notebook is akin to not writing it down at all.

Successful artifact management is the key to avoiding Malcolm events, and the key to successful artifact management are the three As. These are:

Availability: Your artifact matters. You already know that, but does everyone else? It needs to be sitting somewhere where anyone who cares is going to trip over it. It's a wiki page, it's an e-mail sent to everyone, it's a presentation. I don't know what your organization communication patterns are, but you've got to stick your artifact in the middle of it. "Folks, this scribble is our future." This leads us to the next *A*.

Agreement: The reason you created your artifact is because you believe you've identified a critical piece of information, where critical could mean novel, controversial, or just important. By making your artifact available to the team, you're saying, "Pay attention to me," and this is a critical juncture. This is when you consign a Malcolm event to oblivion because you're making it common knowledge. It sounds like I'm just describing availability again, but I'm not. I'm talking about the hallway argument that goes down when Phil reads your weekly status reports and it reads, "We're not doing Phil's favorite feature."

So, you and Phil have it out. You debate pros and cons, he gives a little, you give a little, and suddenly, it's OK. We don't need to do Phil's feature because we're doing this other feature and Phil understands why.

Accuracy: This is the easiest part of the three As. As your artifact soaks through the organization, it's going to change. Folks are going to tweak the scribble, Phil is going to request a minor change, and your artifact is going to evolve. Take the time to revise the artifact as it evolves in the hallway because you never know what minor change might set off some random person who was fine with the first version of the artifact.

Availability, agreement, and accuracy. I call these nouns "binders" because they bind people to the Malcolm event. If they see, read it, and comment on it, it becomes bound to them. It's no longer an insignificant event, it's common knowledge.

Success Is Often Silence

Avoiding Malcolm events is completely unsatisfying and here's why: you know what failure sounds like, but success is silent. It's when the release goes well. It's when you don't have to release an immediate update to your major release. Avoiding a Malcolm event is when you managed to predict the future and no one is going to believe you when you tell them what you did because nothing happened.

Management is the care and feeding of the invisible. You're doing your best when it appears the least is happening. I love the thrill of the last month of a release as much as the next guy, but I suspect the reason we're yelling at each other, working weekends, and feeling the depressing weight of compromise is because we're surrounded by Malcolm events.

Capturing Context

Each organization in a company has their Favorite Application. It's not truly their favorite application; it's just the application they must use in their particular capacity in the organization. Stand up right now and walk into an unfamiliar part of your building and stalk your coworkers. If someone stops and asks you what you're doing, tell them, "Rands sent me," and vigorously nod your head. That always works.

As you walk the hallways of this strange new part of your organization, look at their screens. What's the consistent application sitting on their monitors? Is it Excel? Well, you're probably in some area of operations. Are you seeing a lot of Word? Maybe legal, possibly tech pubs. Is the cube empty? That's sales.

The most common application in engineering is an editor. Whether it's a terminal window or the world's fanciest integrated development environment, their Favorite Application is a code editor, but it's not their secret weapon . . . that's version control.

The concept behind version control is simple. It's a central network repository for all the files of which a project is comprised. If I want to edit a file, I run a tool (which works alongside my editor) that makes a local read/write copy of that file on my system. I make my changes and then, using the same tool, I check in my file to the network. So, what's the big deal?

Usually, there is no deal. You merrily check in and check out your files with no fuss. The deal occurs when you realize that software projects are often massive collections of files that are edited by teams of people. A version control system solves the problem that occurs when two engineers have checked out and have changed the same file at the same time. Whoever checks in their changed file first has no deal. When the second one checks in, that engineer receives a message that warns, "Hey, this file has changed while you had it checked out. Whaddayawannado?" The user then gets to figure out how to merge the two files into a consistent working whole.

That's version control as a traffic cop and that's cool because it prevents folks from bonking each other on the heads, but I haven't gotten to the major cool, and that's the other thing I do when I check in. I don't just check the file in; I also include information about what I changed:

"Rands added a new blingleforth function. It rocks."

The version control server then copies my new version of the file up, tags the new version with my name and my comments, and increments the version number associated with the file.

Let's ignore the useful fact that every single version of the file is stored in this system and focus on the comment I included with this change. This is the big deal. This is the secret weapon in engineering. We not only save every version of our work, we also capture the context of the change. Version control stores the thoughts that made our ideas bright.

If you're thinking, "My, what a quaint nerd custom," if you're not having a clouds-are-parting moment, think about two products: del.icio.us and Flickr. Both have built their feature sets around capturing context, and by context, I do mean tags. Each time someone adds a new link or photo to these services, they can add whatever tags they like. No rules. Just start typing words regarding what makes the link or photo relevant. That's context.

When you start stumbling around Flickr and del.icio.us, you realize the value that is created when people choose to capture and share the context of their content. At the South by Southwest Interactive conference in Austin, I was in awe of the folks who were taking the time not only to capture and upload their photos to Flickr, but also taking the time to carefully tag all their content. Thirty minutes after a presentation, there were dozens of tagged pictures sitting in Flickr for the presentation I just watched.

So What?

Think of the big project you're working on right now. For me, it's this chapter. I'm merrily typing away and hitting the Save button every 12 seconds because I'm a twitchy saver. Comes from years of flaky Windows applications that liked to crash. *If you save a lot, you're not screwed.*

When should I capture context on this project? When should I stop and capture the thoughts about what I just wrote? Whenever I've created significance. I've been keeping track of these moments while I've been writing and so far; they are:

1. New intro down, borrowed from version control article I can never seem to finish.

2. Removed Wikipedia from example technology—Flick'n'del.icio.us are enough . . . don't confuse them with wikis.

3. Keep moving disclosure paragraph around . . . haven't found a home, yet. Might be wrongly in love with this paragraph.

Do these comments matter to you? No. Do they matter to me? Yes. Do I want my favorite editor to prompt me every time I hit the Save key for context? No. I want another verb, let's call it *wow*, and let's have it mean, "I've done something significant to my project and I want to capture the context of that change."

This is not an obvious activity for most people. In fact, huge passive-aggressive battles have been fought within my engineering teams over these change comments. It's a fight between those who are lazy and just want to check in their files and those who know that, while having the code safely in version control is good, understanding what is happening to the project on a day-to-day basis is even better. It's called a status report.

That's right; I finally found my technology angle on killing status reports. We need our tools to allow us to capture context at the moment we're being bright, not Friday at 4 p.m. when we're trying to get the hell out of work. How much easier would your status report process be if all you had to do on Friday afternoon was ask your favorite app, "Show me all the wow for the last week"? That report alone is enough incentive for me try to remember to record my wow among all my twitchy saving.

Nerd Disclosure

I'm serious a version control nerd. At Borland, I was the junior engineer, which means I was saddled with building the product duties. This means if the product did not build, someone yelled at me. This gave me a strong incentive to build an application that forced each engineer to make a comment, no matter how small, each time they checked into the project. *It's not me. It's him.* At Netscape, I watched in awe as CVS was merged with bug tracking and build systems via primal web applications. I still drool over Tinderbox. At my startup, I was the guy who took Microsoft SourceSafe out behind the building and kicked the shit out of it.

I live and breathe version control because I see the value. Each year, I learn more about more Favorite Applications. I learn how executives live and breathe presentation software. I learn about the magic that those folks in operations can coax out of Microsoft Excel. Everyone is hard at work creating stuff, and, with some minor tweaks to our Favorite Apps, we can wrestle version control from the nerds and help everyone index their brightness.

Status Reports 2.0

At a startup, there are two organizational inflection points that drastically change communication within the organization. The first occurs around 50 or so people. This is the moment when, if you're an early employee, you see someone in the hallway that you don't recognize.

This is troubling. Until that point, not only did you know everyone on a first-name basis, but you also knew what they were about, what they were responsible for, and what floated their boat. Now, there's an unknown quantity in the building.

This awkward but necessary evolution of the organization passes. You accept the fact that the company is growing and you decide to focus your attention just on your group. Who cares what those schmoes over in the support group are doing anyhow? You've got an engineering organization to build.

The second inflection point happens somewhere around 200 people. The situation that began during the first inflection point is now a serious problem. As the individual groups have grown, fiefdoms have been created in the organization and they're not talking to each other because they're focused on their own internal growth. What made your organization great early on—efficient communication—is still going on. It's just going on inside of each of your groups and not across them.

Someone, usually an executive type with business in these different fiefdoms, is going to recognize this.

They're going to have two meetings on the same topic with different groups. When they're done, the executive is going to panic. He's going to realize that these two groups have no clue what the other is up to, and, more importantly, they have no desire or incentive to figure it out.

Executive panic means an offsite where all of management gets together to redefine goals, communication, and teamwork. When everyone gets back, someone gets promoted to director to help glue the different organizations back together. As for improving communication, well, the common knee-jerk reaction is to curse the organization in the form of status reports.

I've managed a variety of different-sized organizations. In the larger ones, inevitably, I've had a meeting with my managers where I've needed to explain what my status report policy is. I've always started this conversation with the same preface: "I'm sorry, but we've got to do status reports."

Why am I apologizing? Clear communication is a good thing and status reports are just good, clean communication, right? No, they're not. The reason I'm apologizing is because by instituting or supporting a status report policy, I'm admitting, "I do not have a better solution for facilitating good communication than busywork in the form of status reports. Sorry, I'm pathetic."

The idea of status reports is not a bad one. Generally, I ask for the following information on a weekly basis: highlights, lowlights, and any open issues. Pretty simple. Think of it as a weekly litmus test.

The first few weeks with a new group, I tend to get stellar status reports from the team. Lots of detail, lots of energy, and lots of content. It's clear that the manager and the team spent time on the report.

Two months later. Dullsville. The very same people who were generating content-rich status reports are now sending bulleted lists that really don't change on a weekly basis. I stop reading them, they stop writing them, and we're back in the Land of Poor Communication where we perpetuate the fact that everyone hates status reports.

This needs to be fixed.

Know Your Audience

There are two major consumers of status reports. The first consumers are managers and executives. These are the folks who want a high-level overview of where all the money is going. You want to keep this group in the loop not only because they sign the checks, but also because they are the major influencers within the organization. Keeping them abreast of current drama in your organization is essential when you're preparing them for that two-month slip to improve quality.

Due to the fact that these folks see a lot of status reports, there's a requirement for the data to be somewhat normalized because you don't want them getting frustrated figuring out where the relevant information is; you want them acting on it. And they want to. Managers who have been staring at status reports for a decade are very good at picking up warning signs from seemingly inconsequential updates within them.

The other major consumer of status reports is, well, everyone else in the company. Actually, let me rephrase. The other consumer is everyone else in the company who needs to read your status report. I'll explain.

Right now, you send your status report to a group of people or a mailing list that goes to "the right people." The definition of "right people" is likely based on roles in the organization, management, leads, and whoever is supposed to have cross-functional visibility into whatever it is that you do.

Here's the problem with that audience.

Let's say you've had an open issue on your status reports for four weeks now. It's gone on long enough that your manager is starting to bring up your issue at your one-on-one and she's getting frustrated that your answer to "What progress has been made?" is *shrug*. The correct answer to your four-week open issue is sitting in the head of Joe Blow engineer who sits nowhere near you. He's completely outside of your management food chain and he can save you weeks of effort and possible executive embarrassment. How in the world are you going to get to this guy?

Sure, if you've got a bright list of dynamic individuals on your recipient list for your status report, there's a good chance that someone might make the connection between your open issue and Joe Blow, but, chances are the manager has grown jaded about status reports, *just like you*.

The Three-Tiered Fix

You're waiting for the punch line here. You think I've got a solution to fix status reports, and, well, I might, but it mostly depends on you insisting on a change.

I've got a three-tiered strategy for fixing status reports, and I know that you're translating "three-tiered" into "lots of work," and, yeah, it is, but you're a manager and your job is not just the management of people, it's the management of information.

Our first tier is, in my opinion, the most useful. What you're going to do is set up a wiki for your group. Nothing fancy, there's a ton of them out there. With this wiki in hand, you're going to start to insist that interesting pieces of documentation stop being uselessly sent around via e-mail and be placed in the wiki. You are the evangelist. Your first answer to any question regarding information should be, "Check the wiki," and if the answer to that question is "It's not there," your answer is "Add it." Feature specifications, how-to documents, anything of value that is slowly gathering dust in your inbox needs to live in the wiki.

The goal with the wikification of your group is not only to create an information repository for the team, but also to get them into the practice of using it. Their mental process when they need to find something out shouldn't first be "Who should I bug?" it should be "I wonder if it's in the wiki? And if it's not, why not?" I'm a fan of teams bugging each other for information, but if it's critical information, why doesn't it live somewhere where acquiring it doesn't involve me stopping whatever it is I'm doing to dig through my inbox three times a week?

Now, you're thinking we haven't touched on the status report issue yet, but we have. Once you've established your wiki as the de facto standard for information about your group, it's going to spread. When another team needs a piece of information from your team and they get forwarded a URL to the wiki, they're bookmarking it, and each bookmark of your wiki increases its value inside of the organization. With a little consistent persistence on your part, your wiki isn't going to replace the need for a status report, but it is going to create a virtual presence for your team. Your wiki should be the recognized source of pipin' hot information in your group, and the sooner that happens, the sooner Joe Blow is going to stumble across your hard problem.

Once you've established the wiki as your informational home, it's time to get the team to start posting their statuses there as well. Some folks choose to use a weblog for this, but a wiki works fine, too. The weblog has the advantage of being both organized in reverse chronological order, which puts the latest news at the top of the page, and a self-publishing platform; individuals own their content—as opposed to a wiki, where anyone can edit anything. Both of these are minor technical advantages and less important than you insisting that status is posted regularly and in a public place for everyone to see.

Yeah, everyone. I've been in many organizations where managers see the information contained within a status report as confidential or secret, and this baffles me. By making your status reports open to public scrutiny, you're going to find that first, they're easier to find. Second, status report writers, knowing they have a larger audience, are going to work harder on status reports knowing it's not just for you. It's for the entire company.

Lastly and most depressing, you still need to send that regular e-mail to senior management. I know I told you I wanted to fix the dull mundanity of status reports, and here I am suggesting that you keep on sending the same old e-mail, but you're not. If you've insisted on your wiki being the primary source of information for your team, and team members are consistently sharing their status via weblogs, well, you've solved a couple of key problems.

First, everyone on the team is spending less time keeping the rest of the organization apprised of what your team is doing because they're no longer answering e-mails and instant messages all week, they're just pointing people at the wiki.

Second, by getting more information to more people, you're helping the organization communicate more efficiently. I love sitting in a meeting with a group of random coworkers giving an update, and one of them chimes in, "Uh, Rands, isn't this information in your wiki?"

You bet it is.

Third, and lastly, the process by which you gather the information for your status reports should be easier because it is sitting there in weblogs waiting to be massaged into your next report.

And you need to send it. Consistently.

It needs to be pushed by you to the executives not because they're too busy to pull it, but because this document defines what you do and how you're doing it. The regular delivery of this information is an intelligent reminder; it's a press release for your team. "We're here. We're working hard and there's more to do."

Trickle Theory

Buried.

Back at the startup, we were shifting gears. After six months of talking about shipping a product, we needed to ship a product, and nothing gets everyone's attention like a deadline. The good news was that QA had been doing its job, and there was a pile of work in our bug database. The bad news was that no one had looked at the database in months.

We had a rent-a-VP at the time, and as temporary executives go, he was sharp. He quickly deduced our goal—ship a quality beta—but he also quickly discerned that we had no idea about the quality of the product because of our pile of untriaged bugs.

He called a meeting with the QA manager, the tech support manager, and me. His advice: "Triage every single bug in this fashion and tell me how many bugs we've got to fix in order to ship this beta." And then he left.

Every single bug. 537 bugs. You gotta read the bug, possibly reproduce it, and then make an educated team decision. Let's assume an average of 5 minutes per, and you're talking about . . . crap . . . 45 hours of bug triage. It's an impossible task. I've got features to fix, people to manage, and I haven't seen the sun on a Saturday in two weeks.

Let's take a brief segue and talk about the huge value that exists in a bug database. In just about every company I've worked at, the only source of measurable truth regarding the product is the bug database. Marketing documents get stale. Test plans become decrepit. Test case databases slowly mutate into the unusable personal to-do list of QA. The bug database is the only source of data regarding your product.

I know this. I know that once I've effectively scrubbed the bug database, I've got the single most informed opinion regarding the product.

But.

537 unscrubbed bugs? 40-plus hours of bug drudgery?

Please. I've got a product to ship.

My normal approach when faced with an impossible task is analysis because analysis gives you data, which in turn allows you to make a confident decision. So, I do what I did above: carefully estimate how long it will take to complete . . . 5 minutes $\times$ 537 = impossible. This fair estimate freezes me with fear. How in the world am I going to get my other five jobs done while scrubbing 40 hours of bugs? Once I'm good and lost in that fear, the impossible task, I'm no longer thinking abut getting the task done, I'm thinking about the fear.

My advice is: Start.

"But Rands . . . I've got 300 tests to run and one day to . . ."

Stop. Go run one test. Now.

"Wait, wait, wait. Rands. Listen. They need this spec tomorrow at 9 a.m. . . ."

Shush. Quiet. Go write. Just a paragraph. Now.

Welcome to Trickle theory.

Our Villain

My traditional first move when managing impossible tasks is to put the task on a to-do list.

"There! It's on the list. Aaaaaaah . . . didn't that feel good? It's on the to-do list, which must mean it will be done at some point, right?" Wrong. Putting the task on the to-do list does one thing: it avoids *the Critic*.

Every story needs a villain, and in this piece our villain is the Critic. This is your internal voice, which does careful and critical analysis of your life, and he's gained a powerful place in your head because he's saved your butt more than once.

He's the one who told you that offer from the startup smelled too good to be true. You remember that company, right? The one that simply vanished three months after you declined that stunning offer letter. It was the Critic who said, "How in the world can they afford to give anyone this type of offer when I don't even understand their business model?"

The Critic was the one who calmed you inner nerd and convinced you to not buy HDTV three years ago, and he told you not to trust that fast-talking engineering manager who emphatically guaranteed his team would be done on schedule. The Critic said, "People who talk fast are moving quickly to cover up the gaps in their knowledge."

The Critic was right. The Critic gained credibility, but for this piece, he's still the villain.

I know it feels great to get that impossible task on the to-do list. I know it feels like you actually did something, but what you've done is avoid conflict. You know that if you start considering the impossible task, the Critic is going to chime in with his booming voice of practicality, "*Rands, what are you thinking? No one adds features two weeks before a ship date!*"

"OK, all right, you're right, but the boss wants it and when the boss gets something in his head it takes a lot of work to blah blah blah . . ." Now, you're justifying, you're worrying, and you're arguing with the Critic when what you should be doing is starting.

Nothing Happens Until You Start

Let's first break down impossibleness. For the sake of this article, there are two types of impossible tasks. First, there are impossibly dull tasks. This is work that requires no mental effort, but is vast in size. Bug scrubbing is a great example of this. At the other end of the spectrum are impossibly hard tasks. These are tasks like, "Hey Rands, we need a new product by Christmas. Yes, I know it's October. Ready? Go!"

Oddly, attacking both boring and hard tasks involve the same mental kung fu where your first move is starting.

Such silly, trivial advice . . . start. Still, take a moment and examine your mental to-do list or just look at your written one. How many terribly important tasks have been there more than a month? More than a year? Embarrassing, huh? It's not that they're not important; it's just that you didn't begin and you didn't begin because the moment you think about starting, the Critic weighs in, "How will you even start? You'll never finish! You don' t even know where to start."

Begin. Go read the first bug. Don't think about how many are left. Go to the next one and watch what happens. In just a few minutes, you'll have made something resembling progress. Two more bugs, and it'll start to feel like momentum. Progress + momentum = confidence. The moment you see yourself tackle the smallest part of the impossible task, the quieter the Critic becomes because you're slowly proving him wrong.

Iterate

The second piece of advice is simpler than the first, which is hard to imagine. Iterate. Once you've kicked yourself out of stop, iterate becomes a little easier, but if you're truly tackling an impossible task, the Critic simply isn't going to shut up.

"Wow, you've closed five bugs . . . Only 532 more to go, sport!"

Iteration and repetition aren't going to silence the Critic. Progress will. A beautiful thing happens when you point your brain at an impossible task. Once you've begun and start chewing on whatever the task is, you'll start to see inefficiencies and begin to fine-tune your process. This is how an engineer who tells you, "It's going to take two weeks to write that code" comes back after the weekend and says, "It's done." He honestly believed that it was a two-week task, but as soon as he started chewing on the problem, he realized he'd written similar code a year ago, which, with a half a Saturday of tweaking, provided the same functionality.

The same applies to small, duller impossible tasks. Previously, when I estimated it'd take five minutes of triage for each bug, I didn't take into consideration that after about 50 bugs, I was going to be really good at scrubbing bugs. I'd start to identify people who generally wrote good bugs versus those who didn't have a clue. I'd learn the problematic areas of the product and learn where I could make snap judgments regarding bug viability. What was a 5-minute triage window for the first 50 bugs was 1 minute for the next 50, and that turned into an average of 15 seconds per bug for the second hundred when I really got rolling.

This means that my original estimate of needing 45 hours for bug scrubbage turned out to be roughly 7 hours. What I thought would take a week is actually going to take one solid day.

Do not believe that this gives you the authority to slice every single estimate by five. Turns out that impossible tasks, upon consideration, actually are terrifically hard. Believe this; an individual tends to be very bad at work estimates until they've begun the work.

Mix It Up

Crap. You've been saddled with an impossible task, and after a weekend of no sleep, you have confirmed, yes, the task is impossible. In fact, you've started, you've iterated, and you still have no clue how to actually complete the task. Story time.

This spring I had a crew come up to clear some brush on the property. Now, the property is a pleasant combination of oaks, bays, and redwoods, but much of it had become overgrown and inaccessible. My first thought when I moved in was, "Hell yes, I've got clearing mojo!" My thought after one weekend of clearing, when I was partially successful at clearing up 50 square feet of 5 *acres of forest* was, "Impossibly boring."

This attitude gave me a unique curiosity when the crew of three men showed up, chain-saws in hand, to clear the land. They had no issue starting and they clearly had the iteration thing down, but they also demonstrated the last and most important component to Trickle theory: mix it up.

It went like this: one guy would cut and drag brush into the fire, another would cut trees down, and the third would trim fallen trees. This went on for a while, and then they'd all switch. Now, drag guy was cut guy, cut guy was hauling wood guy, and trim guy was stack guy. During lunch, I sat down and asked, "When do you guys switch jobs?"

"When we're bored."

Beautiful, beautiful Trickle theory. How cool is this? If you're working on an impossibly hard or impossibly dull task and you find yourself mentally blocked by boredom or confusion, stop and do something else. The benefits of stopping are stunning.

First, stopping smacks the Critic squarely across the face. See, he's also the voice in your head saying, "Uh, if we don't work hard on this, we're screwed." And the longer you sit there grinding out the impossible task when you don't want to, the louder he gets.

Second, stopping to do something else is fun for you and your brain. It breaks the cycle of whatever tasks you're doing and points your gray matter at a whole new problem—and your brain loves new; it consumes new with vim and vigor, and that puts spring in your proverbial mental step.

Third, and most important, even though you are stopping, your brain is bright enough to keep background processing the impossible task. This is why we find so much inspiration in the shower; you're stopping and letting your brain wander, and your brain is smart. Your brain knows how important it is to rewrite that feature in two days and your brain is always working on that feature whether you know it or not.

"Wait, wait, wait. Rands, let me get this straight. Your suggestion when I've got a looming impossible deadline is to stop working on my deliverables?"

What I'm saying is, when you're facing an uphill mental battle with yourself regarding the impossible task, it's time to choose another battle . . . that isn't a battle.

Entropy Always Wins

My life appears to be an endless series of tasks that are geared to slightly tidy up my world. Viewed as a whole, these tasks represent a lot of work. Viewed against the actual amount of entropy in play in my small part of the world, these tasks represent a futile effort.

Fact is, your world is changing faster than you'll ever be able to keep up with, and you can view that fact from two different perspectives:

- I believe I can control my world, and through an aggressive campaign of task management, personal goals, and a *can do* attitude, I will succeed in doing the impossible. Go me!

Or . . .

- I know there is no controlling the world, but I will fluidly surf the entropy by constantly changing myself.

Surfing entropy takes confidence. This isn't Tony Robbins confidence; this is a personal confidence you earn by constantly adapting yourself to the impossible.

VERSIONS OF YOU

It's time to get selfish.

In the first two sections of the book, we worried about managing people and products. Now, I want you to worry a bit about yourself before you worry about everyone else. This involves being a little selfish, and that's why the first two chapters of this section appear to have nothing to do with management. They have to do with figuring out how to get your résumé noticed and making sure you don't screw up your phone screen.

After that, I get back on the management wagon and, well, I start calling people names, which is behavior I need to explain.

Most chapter titles come to me well before the piece is written. This is likely because much of my writing starts as part of a coffee-induced high driving to or from work and there is no way I can completely remember my chain-of-consciousness rambly thoughts from when I park the car to when I'm near a keyboard.

So I create a name.

And it needs to be a good descriptive name because I've got to remember 30 minutes of mental wandering just by thinking of it.

This last section is full of just these sorts of names. Inwards, outwards, organics, NADD, free electrons, bellwethers, incrementalists . . . I clearly have name-calling issues, but these names aren't just a handy memory device, they're the end result of years of sitting at a table and noticing and labeling the similarities among very different people.

These names are not intended to paint a complete picture of the people they describe. They merely give you a starting point for understanding where your particular person is coming from. In reality, your free electron is also an organic completionist. In reality, people are messy.

While I'm happy to provide you with a starting mental sketch for identifying the people on your team and in your company, your job isn't done there. Your job is not to figure out how to alienate people by calling them names, it's to figure out how to include them by taking time to understand what they need, and doing your best to give it to them.

You need to remember that everyone is a slightly different version of you.

A Glimpse and a Hook

The terrifying reality regarding your résumé is that for all the many hours you put into fine-tuning, you've got 30 seconds to make an impression on me. Maybe less.

It's unfair, it's imprecise, and there's a good chance that I make horrible mistakes, but there's a lot more of you than me, and while hiring a phenomenal teams is the most important thing I do, I'm balancing that task with the fact that I need to build product and manage the endless stream of people walking into my office.

But here's a glimpse. I'm going to walk you through the exact mental process I use when I look at a résumé. I don't know if this is right or efficient, but after 15 years and staring at thousands of résumés, this is the process.

The First Pass

Your name. It's simple. Do I know you? Whether I do or not, I'm going to immediately Google you to see if I should. Oh, you a have a weblog. Excellent.

Company names. Do I recognize any companies that you worked at? If I do, I don't look at what you actually do, I assume that if I recognize the company, I'm in the ballpark. If I don't know the company, I scan for keywords in the description to get a rough idea. Hmmm . . . networking words. OK, you're a networking guy.

Job description and history. Here I'm looking for history and trajectory. How many jobs have you had and for how long? How long have you been in your current role? Where'd you come from? QA? Or have you always been an engineer? This is when I start looking for inconsistencies and warning flags.

Other interests and extracurriculars. Yeah, this is part of the first pass. I'm eagerly looking to find something that makes you different from the last 50 résumés I looked at. More on this in a moment.

So, we're done. It's been 10 to 20 seconds and I've already formed an opinion. There's a good chance that I've already made a call whether to move forward on you. If there are other folks checking the résumé out, I can certainly be convinced to take a second look, but a basic opinion has been formed.

Before we move to the second pass, let's talk about the parts of your résumé I didn't look at and never will.

Professional objective. This is likely your lead paragraph and I skipped it. Career center counselors across the planet are slamming their fists on their desks as they read this because they've been telling students, "You need to write a crisp career objective. It defines your résumé."

Yes, it does, but I still don't read it and it's not because there isn't good content there, it's the time issue. See, if your résumé is sitting in my inbox, it means someone has already mapped you to an open job in my group. Reading your objective is going to tell me something I already know. Besides, my job title and description scrub will tell me whether we're in the ballpark or not. If I've got a junior engineering position open and you've got ten years' experience, I'll figure out that mismatch when I look at your history.

This doesn't mean you shouldn't include this objective in your résumé. As you'll see below, there's more to the process than just me reading your résumé, and different folks are looking for different content.

Skills. I skip the skills section not only because this is information I'll derive from your job history, but also because this section is full of misinformation. I'm not going to say that people lie in the skills section, but I know that if a candidate has heard the word Linux in the workplace, there's a good chance they're going to put "Familiarity with Linux" as a skill on their résumé.

Besides, again, I know you've goofed around with Linux because you said so in the description of your last job, right?

Summary of qualifications. Similar to skills, this is another skip section for me. Here's a good example from an imaginary résumé: "Proven success in leading technical problem-solving situations." This line tells me nothing. Yes, I know you're trying to tell me that you're strategic, but there is no way you're going to convince me that you're strategic in a résumé. I'm going to learn that from a phone screen and from an interview.

Unlike skills, which I find to be a total waste of time, I will go back to the summary of qualifications if we end up talking. When you write "Established track record for delivering measurable results under tight schedules," I am going to ask you what the hell you mean on the phone and if your answer isn't instant and insightful, I'll know your qualifications are designed to be buzzword-compliant and don't actually define your qualifications.

The Second Pass

If I can't decide whether to schedule a phone screen after the first pass, I go for another. The goal now is, "OK, I saw something I liked in the first pass, is it real?" This is when I do the following:

In-depth job history. I'm going to actually read the job history for the past couple of jobs. Not all of them, just the last two or three. What I'm doing is fleshing out my mental picture of you. I'm looking for more warning flags. Do your responsibilities match your title? How long were you at your most recent job? If it was a long time, can I get a sense of how you grew? If it was short, can I figure out why you left? Do your last two jobs build on each other? Can I get a sense of where you're headed or are you all over the place?

Your job history—your professional experience—is the heart of your résumé. This is where I spent my time vetting you and this is where you should spend your time making sure I'm going to get the most complete picture of who you are and what you're going to bring to my team.

School. Yeah, this is the first time I'll notice whether you went to college or not. I purposely do this because I've found over years of hiring that a name brand university biases my opinion too early. There's a lot to be said for a candidate who gets accepted to and graduates from Stanford or MIT, but I've made just as many bad hires from these colleges as great ones.

Seeing a non–computer science degree is not a warning flag. In fact, I'm a huge fan of hiring physics majors as engineers. For whatever reason, the curriculum for physics has a good intersection with computer science. Any technical major for me is perfectly acceptable, and even non-technical majors with a technical job history make for a résumé worth thinking about.

OK, so that second pass took another 15 to 30 seconds and we're done. You've just given me the opportunity to change your life by potentially bringing you in for an interview and that chance is over. Next!

What's unfair about what just happened is this. You spent hours working on your résumé. You sent it to close friends for review and you edited it. You agonized over the different sections and you stressed about the tone, and here I am, the hiring manager, and I read one-tenth of your work in 30 seconds.

Don't despair. There are some easy things you can do to improve your chances.

Differentiate, Don't Annoy

Design your résumé to downgrade. Your résumé needs to withstand some formatting abuse. Go get your résumé right now and convert it to plain text. Can you still see the different sections? Is your job history still cleanly formatted? Can you still see the different jobs as well as the start and stop dates? Screw around with the margins, too. Where are your line breaks? They'd better not be after every line because that means visual chaos if a well-intentioned recruiter starts messing with fonts.

Never include a cover letter. I don't read them. Recruiters don't pass them on. Make sure the key points of your cover letter are living in your career objective and your job history.

Embrace honest buzzword-compliance. Remember, I'm not the only who is going to read your résumé. I'm likely the most qualified to make a call whether you're a fit for my job, but before your résumé gets to me, it's going to be passed through a couple of different recruiters and these folks are just as busy as I am.

The lifeblood of the recruiter is the keyword. Java, C++, Objective-C. The more specific relevant keywords and buzzwords you can shove into your résumé, there more likely you're going to make it past the initial cut.

As I said above, I skip the skills section because most folks already know that recruiters are just searching for specific words when they're sourcing candidates, so they shove every possible buzzword into their résumé. Know this: if you claim "strong Java background" in your résumé, I'm going to be compelled to figure out how strong your skills actually are. Don't include any keyword or buzzword that you aren't comfortable talking about at length.

Differentiate, don't annoy. You're likely going to start developing your résumé from a template. Maybe you'll use a friend's résumé that you like as a starting point. Excellent. How are you going to make it yours?

Remember, I've looked at thousands of résumés, which means I've seen all the standard templates. I know when you're using Microsoft Word and I know when you've developed a format of your own. Right this second, I'm flipping through a dozen college résumés and the ones I'm spending time on are the ones that grab me visually, where there is something different. On this one, the fellow put a subtle gray box around each of his section headings. On this other one, the candidate used a nice combination of serif and sans serif fonts to grab me.

A couple of subtle visual differences to your résumé goes a long way toward keeping me engaged in reading it, but remember, we're engineers here and efficiency matters. Differentiating your résumé to the point that I can't quickly parse it is going to frustrate me. You're not applying to be a visual designer; you're an engineer. Keep to the standard sections and don't make me work to figure out who you are.

Sound like a human. Here's a doozy, this intern says he "planned, designed, and coordinated engineers' efforts for the development of a mission critical system." Zzzzzzzzzzzzzz. What did this guy actually do? I honestly don't know. Let's call this type of writing style "résumé mumbo jumbo" and let's agree that usage of this style is tantamount to saying nothing at all.

What was the mission critical system? Why was it critical? How in the world did an intern plan, design, and coordinate the engineering efforts? I'm a fan of giving interns real-world work, but it'd take a world-class intern to plan, design, and manage engineers on whatever this mission critical system is.

Take time to write your résumé for a human. You need to hit all the right buzzwords and keywords to get yourself past the layers of recruiters, but I'm the guy who is really going to take apart your résumé, and if you're saying nothing with résumé mumbo jumbo, I'm learning nothing. Give me specifics and give them to me in a familiar tone. I'm not an automaton; I honestly want to know what you do. Tell me a story.

Include seemingly irrelevant experience. This applies mostly to college types who lack experience in high technology. You're going to stress that your job history doesn't include any engineering and you're thinking your summer working at Borders bookstore is irrelevant. It's not. Any job teaches you something. Even though you weren't coding in C++, I want to know what you learned by being a bookseller. Was it your first job? What did you learn about managers? How did you grow from the beginning to the end of the summer? Explain to me how hard work is hard no matter what the job is.

A Glimpse and a Hook

A résumé will never define who you are. It's not the job of your résumé to give me a complete picture, and if you're struggling to include every last detail about who you are, you're wasting your time. Your résumé should be designed to give me a glimpse and a hook.

The glimpse is a view into the most recent years of your professional career. It should convey your three most important accomplishments and it should give me a good idea where your technical skills lie.

The hook is more important. The hook will leave me with a question. Maybe it's something from your "Other Interests" section. How about an objective so outlandish that I can't help but set up a phone screen. I'm not suggesting that you make anything up; I'm asking you to market yourself in a way that I'm going to remember. A résumé is not a statement of facts. It's a declaration of intent.

Nailing the Phone Screen

As we discovered in last chapter, it's almost a miracle when the phone rings and a recruiter wants to set up a phone screen. The fact is, someone, somewhere in the organization has successfully mapped you to an open position. This is a really big deal because, in my experience, the chance that you'll get this job has improved logarithmically. It's not 50/50, but it's vastly better than when you were a random résumé sitting on my desk.

As with last chapter, I'm going to walk you through the precise mental process I go through as part of the phone screen; but before we go there, let's talk motivation.

The Purpose

I've got a requisition, a req. This roughly describes a job I have open in my team, but it's likely not very precise. Job descriptions are notoriously broad and vague because I want to cast the net as wide as possible. It's not just that I want to see as many candidates as possible; I want to see as broad a skill set as possible.

This is important to remember as you're scrubbing job opportunities. I know you're stressing, "The job description says five years of Java required, and, well, I only have two." Don't be absurd. There are usually two buckets of skills in a job description: required and recommended. At the very least, you should be in the ballpark for required, but don't give recommended a second thought. It's recommended. It's nice to have.

Besides, you got a phone screen with me, so I'm already pretty sure that you're close to a fit, but I still have questions, otherwise I would've just brought you in. The question is, what questions do I have? Guess what—your job is to figure that out.

Your Job Is to Prepare

Before you even talk to me, you're on a fact-finding mission. You've got a job description, and after the phone screen has been set up, you've got my name. You might also have an idea of the product or technology associated with this gig, or you might not, but even without a product name, you've got plenty of information to start with.

Do your research. Google me. Find out anything you can about what I do and what I care about. This isn't stalking, this is your career, and if I happen to be an engineering manager who writes a weblog, well, you can start to learn how I think. Maybe I don't have a weblog but I post to mailing lists. That's data, too. How is this going to help you during the phone screen? Well, I don't know what you're going to find, but anything you can gather is going to start to build context around this job that you know nothing about. This helps with nerves as well. See, I have your résumé and you have nothing. A bit of research is going to level the information playing field.

If you have a product name or technology, repeat the same process. What is the product? Is it selling well? What do other people think about it? I'm not talking about a weekend of research here; I'm talking an hour or so of background research so that you can do one thing when the phone screen shows up: you need to ask great questions.

That's right. In your research, you want to find a couple of compelling questions, because at some point during the phone screen I'm going to ask you, "Do you have any questions for me?" and this is the most important question I'm going to ask.

Back to the Beginning

Before I ask you the most important question, I need to figure out a couple of things. First, in a perfect world, we'd be able to skip the phone screen and just bring you in for a first round interview, but this rarely happens unless I already know you. What I need to know is:

Can we communicate? I'm going to lead off with something simple and disarming. It's either going to be the weather or something I picked up from your extracurricular activities. "Do you really surf? So do I! Where do you surf?" These pleasantries appear trivial, but they're a big deal to me because I want to see if we can communicate. It's nowhere near a deal killer if the pacing of our conversation is awkward, I'll adjust, but how off is it? Are we five minutes in and we still haven't said anything? OK, maybe we have a problem.

One more softball. My follow-up questions will now start to focus on whatever questions your résumé left me with. I've no idea what I'm going to ask because it varies with every single résumé, so my thought is that you should have your résumé sitting in front of you because it's sitting in front of me as well. It's my only source material.

Whatever these follow-up questions are, I'm still figuring out how we communicate. This means you need to focus on answering the questions. It sounds stupid, but if it's not absolutely clear to you what I'm asking, it's better to get early clarification rather than letting me jump in five minutes into your answer to say, "Uh, that's not what I was asking."

See, you and I are still tuning to each other. It's been five minutes, and if we're still not adjusted to each other's different communication styles, I'm going to start mentally waving my internal yellow flag. It doesn't need to be eloquent communication, but we should be making progress.

No more softballs. We're past the softball phase of the interview and now I'm going to ask a hard question. This isn't a brainteaser or a technical question, this is a question that is designed to give you the chance to tell me a story. I want to see how you explain a complex idea over the phone to someone you don't know and can't see.

Again, who knows what the actual question will be, but you need to be prepared when I ask that question that is clearly, painfully open-ended. I'm not looking for the quick, clean answer; I'm looking for a story that shows me more about how you communicate and how you think. Being an amazing communicator is not a part of most engineering jobs, I know this. I'm not expecting Shakespeare, but I am expecting that you can confidently talk about this question because I found this question in your résumé, which is the only piece of data we currently have in common. If we can't have an intelligent discussion about that, I'm going to start wondering about the other ways we aren't going to be able to communicate.

Your turn. We're 20 minutes into the phone screen and now I'm going to turn it over to you when I ask, "Do you have any questions for me?"

When I tell friends that this is my favorite question, the usual response is, "So, you're lazy, right? You can't think of anything else to ask, so you go for the path of least resistance." It's true. It an easy question for me to ask, but it is essential because I don't hire people who aren't engaged in what they're doing. And if you don't have a list of questions lined up for me, all I hear is: *You don't want this job.*

A well-thought-out question shows me that you've been thinking about this job. It shows me you're already working for it by thinking about it outside of this 30-minute conversation. Yeah, you can probably wing it and ask something interesting based on the last 20 minutes, but the impression you're going to make with me by asking a question based on research outside of this phone screen will make up for a bevy of yellow flags. It shows initiative and it shows interest.

The Close

And we're done. It went by pretty quick, but the question is, "How'd it go?" Here's a mental checklist to see how you did:

Long, awkward pauses. Were we struggling to keep things moving? Were there long silences? Well, we didn't tune appropriately. Again, not a deal killer, but definitely a negative.

Adversarial interactions. What happened when we had different opinions? Did we talk through it or did we start butting heads? This happens more than I expect on phone screens, and it's not always a bad thing. I'm not interested in you telling me what I want to hear, but if we are on opposite sides of the fence, how do we handle it? If a candidate is willing to pick a fight in a 30-minute phone screen, I'm wondering how often they're going to fight once they're in the building.

How'd it feel? This is the hardest to quantify, but also the most important. Did we click? Did the conversation flow? Did we both learn something? Ideally, I'm a decent representation of the culture of the team I'm hiring for, so if the 30 minutes passed painfully, I'm wondering what kind of pain hiring you might inflict on the team.

Specific next steps. How did I leave it? Did I give you a song and dance about how "we're still interviewing candidates and we'll be in touch within the next week"? Well, that's OK, but what you're really looking for is a specific next step like "I'm going to bring you in" or "Let's have you talk with more of the team." An immediate and actionable next step is the best sign of success with a phone screen. If I don't give you this as part of the close, ask for it. If I stall, there's a problem.

Like your résumé, the goal with the phone screen is to convince a single person to move forward with hiring you. With your résumé, you send your hope to an anonymous recruiting e-mail address. With a phone screen, you have leverage. It's not the 30-minute window that you need to worry about, you need to worry about how you're going to prepare.

The phone screen is the first time you get to represent yourself as a person, not some résumé sitting on my desk. It's still a glimpse, but it's the first time you can actively participate in the process.

CHAPTER

22

Ninety Days

When you accept a new job, you don't know who you are going to work with, what you are going to be doing, and how much (or little) you're going to like it. Call everyone you want. Ask their opinions. Trust the fact that a good friend referred you for the gig. Revel in the idea that the company has a good pedigree, but don't delude yourself that in a smattering of interview hours you're going to have anything more than a vague hint of your new life.

Try this. Tell me about your best friend. Give me a bulleted list of five noteworthy things you think I should know about your best friend. Got it? Read it out loud. Does this do justice to your best friend? I hear you when you say, "He'd do anything for me," but why is that? Why is he protective of you? What's the story behind the bullet? That's what I want to know.

Each person in your new team has a story they want to tell you and it's never a bulleted list. Some are going to freely give this story whereas others will carefully protect the fact they even have a story, but until each person you need to work with has shared this story with you (and vice versa), the interview isn't over. The jury is out and you won't know if this new job that you've begun is actually your job.

Deliberation

Your first job is to relax. Like the first day of school, you're going to overcompensate in your first day, your first week. Most people do not lay their clothes out the night before they go to work. You're doing this to calm yourself. Those clothes neatly laid out at the end of your bed are a visual reminder that you have control over this thing that you can't control.

Relax. There's an industry standard regarding the amount of time it takes to make a hire, and it's 90 days. New managers hate when I tell them this because they're so giddy they've got a new requisition and, *boy, watch how fast I can hire*. Yes, yes. I appreciate your velocity, but I'm not going to worry about your hire for 90 days.

This chunk of time applies to your new job as well. You've got 90 days—3 months—to finish your job interview. Draw an a X on a calendar 90 days from now. Make it a physical act that reminds you to relax and to listen rather than fret about what you don't know. The new team isn't going to trust you until you stop laying out your clothes, until you stop being deliberate.

I know you've done this before: you've had five other jobs and you have well-refined people-assessment instincts. Except, well, they're biased. These instincts are based on where you've been and you have never been here before. My suggestion is that the less you trust your instincts, the more you'll learn about your new job, and that's why I wrote you a 90-days list . . . .

1. Stay Late, Show Up Early

You need a map of the people you work with, and I find the best way to start scribbling this map is to understand people and their relation to the day. When do they get there? How long until they engage in what they do? Coffee run? Wait, no. Late arriver. Doesn't leave until he gets something done. Makes his coffee run at 4:30 p.m. Doesn't drink coffee? Really? Why? These long days of watching give you insight, and they give you tools for understanding what each of your team members want.

2. Accept Every Lunch Invitation You Get

People are stretching themselves for you the first few weeks you show up. They're going to go out of their way to include you, and no matter who they are, you've got to take the time to reciprocate. The lunch invite from that guy in the group you're pretty sure you'll never interact with will result in stories, and you have a stunning lack of stories right now.

3. Always Ask About Acronyms

It's great that we're all speaking English, but why is it that you're sitting in your first staff meeting and not understanding a word? It's because every team develops acronyms, metaphors, and clever ways to describe their uniqueness, which you must understand. Cracking the language nut is absolutely essential to assessing the hand you've been dealt, and you're going to need to ask a couple of times.

4. Say Something Really Stupid

Good news, you're going to do this whether it's on this list or not. I'm saying it's OK. This stupid thing that you're going to say is going to demonstrate your nascent engagement in your job and when they stop giggling, the team is going to know you're desperately trying to figure it all out.

5. Have a Drink

Similar to the lunch task, but more valuable. No barrier is crossed when someone invites you to lunch, but when you get the drink invite, someone is saying, "C'mon. Let's go try a different version of honesty." Stories are revealed over drinks, not lunch.

> **WARNING** The next three on the list are at the bottom for a reason. These are advanced moves that you don't want to attempt until you've built some confidence that if they go horribly wrong, you have some assurance that you won't permanently damage your still-developing reputation. Read on.

6. Tell Someone What to Do

Everything I've talked about so far involves listening and asking questions. This task involves you saying something. More importantly, it involves you telling someone what to do. I don't know who you're telling or what you're saying, but the goal is to exert your influence, to test your influence. More importantly, to test your knowledge of the organization and see if this thing you have to say is true. Telling is the sound of your instincts aligning to this particular organization and this thing you are saying is your first bit of inspiration. Trust it. Tell the right person and realize that everyone was waiting for you to say it.

7. Have an Argument

This is the riskiest item on the list, but potentially the most revealing. There's a good chance when you pull a number 6 that this is going to happen anyway. Again, what you are willing to argue about and who is going to be on the other side of the argument is a function of your situation. What you want to understand is, how does the organization value conflict? Is it OK that you're digging your heels in? Do others engage in the argument? Who swoops in to save the day? Can these people argue without losing their shit? Does this team argue out in the open or do they use devious passive-aggressive subtlety?

You're going to learn two valuable things during this professional battle. First, how does this group of people make a decision? Second, you're going to have a better taste of their passion and their velocity.

8. Find Your Inner Circle

In your arguments, lunches, drinks, and late nights, you're going to find kindred spirits. This is the short list of people who share your instincts. These are the ones who complete your sentences and they know your stories. These are the ones who welcome the argument because they know great decisions are made by many. Your inner circle is not exclusive because you'll go nowhere drawing relationship boundaries among the team. This is the list of people with whom you share your raw inspiration and your stories because you know they'll gleefully help refine them.

The discovery of your inner circle won't happen until time has passed. You'll instinctively be attracted to people who feel comfortable, who feel right, but they can't be in the inner circle until they've passed the test of time. They've got to pass through the 90-day list a few times before you've heard enough stories to let them in.

Finishing the Interview

It's not just that you forgot to ask key questions during your initial interview process; it's that the person you were walking into that interview as isn't who you are. You're a résumé, you're a referral, and you're a reputation.

Your job interview isn't over until you've asked all the questions and heard all the stories.

Your job interview isn't over until you understand the unique structure that has formed around this particular group of people. It's not just the organizational chart, it's the intricate personalities that have settled into a comfortable, complex communication structure.

Your job interview isn't over until you have a framework for how you are going to interact with these people, and that means understanding not only their goals, but also their invaluable personal quirks. What they tell you the first week has more to do with the fact that you're new than what they actually feel. What they tell you after 90 days is the truth.

Your job interview isn't over until you've changed to become part of a new team.

Bellwethers

Let's start by not deluding ourselves. Hiring anyone is a risk. Google is famous for the intense and lengthy scrutiny they put their candidates under. The Google interview might be intense, but when they decide to hire, they're rolling the dice.

You're not going to know who you hired for months.

This doesn't mean you can't improve your odds.

For me, success in an interview is extracting as much information as possible from the candidate. This doesn't happen because you've got a compelling set of interview questions; it comes from throwing a wildly different set of interviewers at your candidate. What these people find, through their diversity of perspective, is the best information you can have to make a hiring decision.

The Core Interview Team

There are two key groups that need to be paraded by your candidate, and the first one should be obvious, but it's often screwed up. Everyone on the team needs to interview every candidate. I'm going to repeat myself since Dave the Curmudgeon Engineer keeps telling you that he's not interested in interviewing, but he's got to be on the list. Every time.

Interviewing is a team sport and failing to get everyone's perspective regarding a candidate is not only a lost opportunity in terms of gathering some random piece of perspective, but it also sends an implied message to the team when Dave gets excused. The message is, "Dave's opinion doesn't matter." Now combine that message with the question you should be asking yourself, "Why doesn't Dave care about the people he might be working with?" and you've got more than enough reason to insist that everyone on the team interviews candidates.

The other key interview group is trickier. This is your go-to set of interviewers that you trust. They are your *bellwethers*, and when they give a candidate a thumbs down, it's over.

Your bellwether team is where you gather the most perspective. The coworker interviews are going to find some informational gems, and their opinions will greatly affect your decision to hire, but bellwethers are your constant. When they tell you, "This guy is going to change the face of your team," you believe them because they are rarely wrong.

There are three key bellwethers I have for each interview.

Technical

In software development, this is the most obvious skill that needs to be assessed, but it's also the one that is done the worst. Engineers are great at being technical, but they aren't great at being social. This means that there's a good chance the best engineer on the team might be the worst technical interviewer because he's uncomfortable dealing with human beings. This means that when you send him in to figure out whether your candidate knows anything about database normalization, he's going to be more nervous than the candidate about asking a hard technical question.

Find a technical bully.

Yes, there are lots of valuable things to learn about communication style, vision, and personality, but if you're an engineering manager and you can't assess technical ability, you're screwed. You're going to be hiring smooth-talking QA guys who don't know how to code. Whoops.

Finding your technical bellwether is easy. Who technically scared the hell out of you when you interviewed? If you're a manager and didn't get asked technical questions, go wandering around other engineering groups and find the bully. He's there. He knows his stuff and has no issue with figuring out whether your candidate does as well.

Cultural

Your second bellwether is cultural. They've got two aspects of the candidate that they need to assess. First, cultural fit within the team, and second, cultural fit within the company. This gets into the fuzzy world of understanding personalities and that means it's going to be easier to find your technical bellwether than your cultural one because technical ability is quantifiable. "Yes, this guy is a C++ god." The next question is, "OK, so he's a god; is he going to piss off the rest of the team by being godlike?"

A cultural fit is a team fit. Ideally, your team is a functioning unit right now and your next hire should support that function rather than detract from it.

Your cultural bellwether is the person on the team who is going to tell you, "This guy is going to add, not detract." Who you're looking for in your bellwether is the person who best represents the soul of the team. This is the person who can figure out your candidate.

Vision (Strategic or Tactical?)

Your last bellwether vets vision. Their job is to figure out the trajectory of the candidate. Are they up and coming? Do they want to change the world? Have they carved out a safe little corner of technology that is all theirs? I don't know who you need on your team, but you do, and you need to know whether the person you're hiring is strategic or tactical.

A strategic hire is someone who is going to push their agenda, their opinion. They are actively engaged in what they are doing, networking with others who do it, and they'll tell anyone, at length, about how they're going to do it. Strategic hires are going to piss people off because of the annoying intensity of their agenda.

A tactical hire is a person who is filling a well-defined need. "We need a database guy." Like strategics, tacticals know their stuff, but that's all that they know. Also, they're not that interested in pushing an agenda. They just want to get their work done in relative silence.

I'm making no judgment regarding whether strategic or tactical is a better hire for you because I don't have a clue who you're hiring. What's important is to understand what type of vision you need for your hire, and, more importantly, who the right person is to interview for this ability. My preference is that the manager is the person who is the bellwether for vision because that's their job for the group. It's not just that you know what the team needs, it's that vision defines career path and you need to know, as early as possible, what it's going to take to keep a future hire engaged. A strategic isn't going to be with your team long because you simply don't move fast enough, whereas a tactical is going to be happy as long as you keep the work relevant and constant.

Team Consensus

Once the team and the bellwethers have interviewed your candidate, it's time to gather everyone together and hear what they think. This is another time when eager managers try to save time by having the interviewers send their feedback via mail or grab an opinion in the hallway.

Wrong. You always have an interview feedback meeting. The ultimate choice to hire is the hiring manager's, but everyone who takes the time to interview the candidate has a vote, and while they walk out of the interview with an opinion, they haven't really voted until they've heard everyone's feedback.

Watch what happens. Gather everyone together and go around the table. For each person who gives their feedback, take notes and notice, as each person talks, how folks who already talked continue to add more information, and, sometimes, even change their opinion. What you're seeing happen in this meeting is consensus building. Opinions are being shaped by information, but the group is also coming to a collective decision. This is why every team member needs to be on the interview schedule. While it's your decision to hire, you'd be a fool not to follow the lead set by the team.

Be a Fool

There are times when you need to be a fool, and this is when the right hire intentionally isn't a fit for the team. This is another area where your bellwethers may prove more useful than the team's opinion. At my prior gig, we had a curmudgeon architect who, while talented, was creating an aura of negativity in the group. It was the curmudgeon's opinion spilling over on the rest of team, and after two years, it needed an adjustment.

Looking for fresh blood and new perspective, I began recruiting from local universities. My cultural bellwether was one of the first engineers I'd hired, but for this position I went to another engineering manager I admired and asked, "Who is the best person to interview for the culture of your team?"

"That'd be Frank."

Frank became my cultural bellwether because I wanted to change the culture of the team. As we brought college hires through the interview process, the feedback meetings weren't surprising. "He's too young! He doesn't know about this technology! We've got too much to do to bring this green person up to speed." This was the existing engineering team taking its content and cultural cues from the senior curmudgeon, and it wasn't surprising that Frank's feedback consistently contradicted the rest of the team. "He's bright. Good fit for the culture and I want to work with this kid."

You're thinking that contradicting the team's consensus opinion on a hiring decision is a downside to the group feedback meeting. It's not. While you need to take special care to explain your decision to each person on the team, you can use the team's consistent negative feedback as part of your reasoning and part of your explanation.

"You remember that feedback? You remember the yelling? Yeah, I'm tired of the yelling, aren't you?"

Still Delusional

We're still deluding ourselves. Even with three of the best bellwethers you can find, hiring anyone is a huge risk. The idea that you can successfully profile a candidate in a phone screen and two rounds of interviews is absurd. All you are getting is a taste. I know you asked them, "How do you deal with stressful situations?" but the fact is you won't actually know who they are until some real stress shows up.

You need to hire. You need to be able to grow your team and that means taking a risk on these people who are a little more than a résumé and some good conversation. While I believe a solid set of bellwether and team interviews is the best means of gathering in-person data about a candidate, don't stop there. Go read their weblog. Find out if they've contributed to open source. Read their posts to mailing lists. In-person interviews are going to give you a glimpse of a person, but anything you can do to complete the picture won't only give you a better perspective, it will reduce the risk that you're hiring a stranger.

NADD

The gist of the book *Guns of the South* is straightforward, yet odd. What if, during the Civil War, the South became equipped with a lot of AK-47s? Long story very short, they would have won. Handily. The author, Harry Turtledove, chose not to focus on time travel or other delectable science fiction tidbits; he spends the time on, "Yay! The South won! So, uh, what are they going to do about that whole slavery thing?"

While I'm certain Civil War enthusiasts would enjoy this book, it is not geared for someone with my particular disability: nerd attention deficiency disorder, or NADD. While I read this book, this innocuous condition reared its head when it became clear that it was an in-depth exploration of the lifestyles and morality during an alternative post–Civil War period . . . ZzZzZzzZZzz.

Now, *Guns* is a fine read, but more than once I was flipping ahead through the pages wondering, "OK, how long is this chapter?" When I neared the end of the book and it became clear that some time traveler from the future wasn't going to appear and, using some whizbang futuristic device, join the North and South together, well, I was disappointed. Sure, I'm happy that President Lee learned his lesson and started abolishing slavery on his own, but . . . no lasers? Please.

Folks, I'm a nerd. I need rapid-fire content delivered in short, clever, punchy phrases. Give me Coupland, give me Calvin and Hobbes, give me Asimov, give me the Watchmen. I need this type of content because I'm horribly afflicted with NADD.

If you're still with me, it might mean you also suffer from some type of NADD-related disorder. Let's find out.

Stop reading this book right now and walk over to your desktop. How many things were you doing when you were last there? Me, I've got a terminal window session open to a chat room, I'm listening to music, I've got Safari open with three tabs where I'm watching stocks on E°TRADE, I'm tinkering with a web site, and I'm looking at weekend movie returns. Not done yet. I've got iChat open, ESPN.com is downloading sports trailers in the background, and I've got two notepads open where I'm capturing random thoughts for later integration into various to-do lists. Oh yeah, I'm rewriting this chapter as well.

Folks, this isn't multitasking. This is an advanced case of nerd attention deficiency disorder. I am unable to function at my desktop unless I've got, at least, five tasks going on at the same time. If your count comes close, you're probably afflicted as well. Most excellent.

A Nerd Diagnosis

My mother first helped diagnose me with NADD. It was the late '80s and she was bringing me dinner in my bedroom (nerd). I was merrily typing away to my friends in some primitive chat room on my IBM XT (super nerd), listening to music (probably Flock of Seagulls—nerd++), and watching *Back to the Future* with the sound off (nerrrrrrrrrrd). She commented, "How can you focus on anything with all this stuff going on?" I responded, "Mom, I can't focus without all this noise."

The existence of NADD in your life is directly related to how you've chosen to deal with the media deluge that has accompanied our insatiable thirst for new technology. You've likely gone one of three ways:

1. You've checked out. You don't own a TV and it's unlikely you're even reading this chapter.

2. You enjoy your content in moderation. When I asked you to count the windows on your desktop, you either said, "One, my mail client, to read my incoming e-mail," or you made yourself a note to check this *after* reading this chapter. You probably own a day planner, which you can touch from where you are sitting right now.

3. You surf the content fire hose. Give me tabbed browsing, tabbed instant messaging, music all the time, and TiVO TiVO TiVO. Welcome to NADD.

The presence of NADD in your friends is equally easily detectable. Here's a simple test: Ask to sit down at their computer and start mucking with stuff on their desktop. Move an icon here, adjust a window there. If your friend calmly watches as you tinker away, they're probably NADD-free. However, if your friend is anxiously rubbing their forehead and climbing out of their skin when you move that icon *12 pixels to the right*, there's NADD in the house. *Back away from the computer.*

The Context Switch

You may think the core competency behind NADD is multitasking, and it's true, NADD sufferers are amazing multitaskers, but it isn't their fundamental skill. It's the context switch.

The idea of the context switch is key to understanding NADD and it's a simple concept. In order to focus on something, you need to spend time and energy to get your brain in the right mental state. Think about your Sunday morning reading of the *New York Times*. You've got your coffee, your comfortable pajamas, your couch, and you've got whatever story it is that you're reading. All of this is your context.

Now, halfway through your current story, I'm going to rip the paper from your hands and turn on CNN, which happens to be running exactly the same story that you were just reading.

What. The hell. Just happened?

You just experienced a context switch. It's not a horrible one, since you're luckily experiencing the same story; it's just in a different medium—TV. Talking heads with that annoying scrolling news bar at the bottom of the screen.

Still, it's jarring, right? Forget about why I'm yanking the paper from your hands, I'm talking about the mental shift from reading a story to watching it. It takes time to switch. For you. A healthy NADD sufferer would barely notice the switch. In fact, chances are, they're already digesting their news via random different media right this second.

What separates a NADD sufferer from everyone else is that the context switch is transparent. The mental muscle that drives the context switch is well developed because it's spent a lifetime switching between random streams of data, trying to make sense of a colossal amount of noise to hear what is relevant.

Anyone can multitask. NADD sufferers multitask with deft purpose. They're on a quest of high-speed information acquisition and processing.

Leveraging NADD

I'm making NADD sound like a trait of information-obsessive power freaks, and, well, it is. How else can you deal with a world where media is forced on you at you at every turn? You become very adept at controlling it. There's more good news.

Folks who are not afflicted with NADD think those who are can't focus because—look at us—we're all over the place. *Please stop clicking on things— you are giving me a headache*. Wrong. Those with NADD have an amazing ability to focus when they choose to. Granted, it's not our natural state, and yes, it can take us longer than some to get in the zone (see Chapter 25 for more about the zone), but when we're there—*boy howdy*.

The web is designed with NADD in mind. Whether it's the short burst of information that comprises a weblog or the RSS behind it, which allows me to read *every weblog ever*, the Web knows about NADD. It knows that any good web page is not designed to answer the question "Do you want to learn?" it's "How long do I have your attention?"

NADD can advance your career, if you're in the right career. Ever worked at a startup? Ever shipped software? What are the last few weeks like? We call it a fire drill because everyone is running around like a crazy person doing random, unexpected shit. NADD is the perfect affliction for managing this situation because it's an affliction that reduces the cost of the context switch.

If the building you are currently in is burning to the ground, go find the person with NADD on your floor. Not only will they know where the fire escape is, they'll probably have some helpful tips about how to avoid smoke inhalation, as well as a vast array of likely probabilities regarding survival rates in multistory building fires. How is it this junior software engineer knows all this? Who knows, maybe he read it on a weblog two years ago. Perhaps a close virtual friend of his in New York is a firefighter. Does it matter? He may save your life, or more likely, keep you well informed with useless facts before you are burned to a crisp.

Downsides

I'm making NADD sound like a rosy affliction. There are downsides.

First, it's a lot of work to figure out your personal regimen of digesting the world, and sorry, you are going to miss things. This will annoy you, but it will also drive you incessantly to look for *the next big thing*.

Second, you're going to sound like a know-it-all. Try not to. Most people don't actually know that much random trivia, useless info, obscure facts, assorted news, current events, and complex mathematical formulas. These people are happy without it and simply because you're brimming with the latest and greatest information doesn't mean that everyone is going to want to hear about it.

You're not going to have much patience with those who have not chosen a NADD-like life. Occasionally, you'll attempt to impart your fractured wisdom, only to throw your hands up four minutes later when it's clear, "Crap, they just don't get it." Chances are, they might've gotten it, and you're just afflicted with a disease where your attention span is that of a second grader.

Whether you're afflicted with NADD or not, you need to understand one thing. It's not going away. The generation that invented NADD in the '80s and '90s has been replaced by the generation that never knew a world without it, and they're going to be annoying in their own unique way.

A Nerd in a Cave

The first few days of any significant overseas trip, I'm a jerk. It's not just the jetlag that's poisoning my attitude; it's the lack of context. I get twitchy when I don't know where my stuff is. Combine that with the fact that no one is speaking English, there are two toilets in the bathroom, and I have no idea what time it is, and you can begin to understand why I'm in such a foul mood.

Three days in, I'm sleeping, I know it's called a bidet, and I'm working hard on my Italian "R" and "U" sounds. I'm having fun, but I'm still thinking about my lack of context. I'm thinking about the familiar place I've built so that I can work.

The Cave

I have a cave. It came as part of the house. I didn't paint the walls blood red; they came that way. Most folks who get the tour walk into the cave and gasp at the walls. "They're so dark. How can you think surrounded by this ominous redness?" I nod and grin slightly and shuffle them off to the next room. See, I love my cave. The thick, blood-red walls wrap me in comfort and that is what a cave does.

My cave is my intellectual home. My kitchen is where I eat, my bed is where I sleep, and my cave is where I think. Everyone has some sort of cave; just follow them around their house. It might be a garage full of tools or a kitchen full of cookware, but there is a cave stashed somewhere in the house.

The nerd cave has some specific traits:

A computer on a desk with ready access to the Internet: The fact that a computer without an Internet connection is essentially a very expensive DVD player is a recent development, but the fact is, when I sit down at my MacBook and there is no wireless, I think, "Well, I could play Bejeweled, right?" In the cave, the Internet is the lifeblood. It connects this dark place with the rest of the world.

World-canceling features such as a door or noise-reducing headphones: These features are a nuisance to significant others interested in communication, but I'll get to that in a moment.

A random collection of comforting nerd knickknacks: This varies wildly from nerd to nerd, but there is always at least one object or talisman of nerddom sitting in the cave. I have this white, carved stone polar bear staring at me right now. I think I got it for Christmas. It's been staring at me for ten years now, and each time I sit down in the cave I worry that if the polar bear weren't there . . . I wouldn't be able to write.

Something to drink: This may be my thing, but I can't really settle into the cave without something liquid. Right now, it's a cup of homebrew by Peet's. In the afternoon, it's a glass of water. In the evening, it might be wine or a beer. For me, the drink is a mental pause where I intensely scrutinize the last 30 seconds. What did I just write? What am I trying to say? [sip] OK, back to work.

A well-defined layout: This ties into my NADD (see Chapter 22), but I have deep knowledge of the layout of my cave. Each month, the housecleaners come for a tidying of the house, and each month I walk into my office when they are done and spend 30 minutes adjusting my monitors, relocating my pens, and re-piling my papers. I think it's great that someone is coming to clean the house, but I wish they'd *stop touching my stuff*.

A view: Like the drink, the view is a mental break, an escape to somewhere else that provides a brief alteration of perspective. This is why everyone in the office wants a window. It's not a status symbol, it's an escape. I've seen nerds without a view go to great lengths to create one. My manager at UCSC built a window frame in his subterranean office and put posters from around the world behind it. When I left UCSC, he had a poster of Audrey Hepburn from *Breakfast at Tiffany's*.

It's an ominous name: the cave. It alludes to a dark, damp place where you are likely to be eaten by a grue. The irony is that the purpose of a cave is not to insulate, its purpose is to germinate. I'll explain.

The Zone

Each weekend morning, my process is this: I wake up, walk upstairs, sit down at the computer, and figure out what is happening on the planet. Once I'm comfortable that the sky is not falling, I walk to the kitchen, grind my coffee beans, and begin to boil water. While the water is heating up, I return to my computer and follow up on whatever tidbits tickled my fancy from my first pass. This morning, it was some font research, followed by looking into options for wireless headphones. Turns out, Sony sucks. Go figure. Water's boiling! Back to the kitchen, where I pour hot water into my French press and dig up my favorite ceramic cup. The coffee needs to sit for three minutes, which means back to the computer! OK, so why do Sony headphones suck? Poor sound quality? Bad design? Bit of both, really. Coffee's ready, so one more trip to the kitchen, where I pour the steaming brew into my favorite cup and travel, once more, back to my cave.

It looks like a lot of work, but I do it instinctively. It's a routine designed to do one thing—get me into *the zone*. Much has been written elsewhere about the mental state that is the zone, but I will say this: it is a deeply creative space where inspiration is built. Anything that you perceive as beautiful, useful, or fun came from someone stumbling through the zone.

Once I've successfully traversed my morning routine and have entered the zone, I am *off limits*. I mean it. Intruding into the cave and disrupting the zone is no different than standing up in the middle of the first-ever showing of *The Empire Strikes Back*, jumping up and down, and yelling, "*Darth Vader is Luke's father! Darth Vader is Luke's father!*" Not only are you ruining the mood, you're killing a major creative work.

No, I'm not going to answer the phone. In fact, it's a sure sign of compromised cave design if I can even hear the phone ring. And no, I don't hear you when you walk in and ask if we should go to the park tomorrow. I don't hear you the second time, either. I don't mean I'm ignoring you, because that'd involve using precious brain cycles I need for the zone . . . I really *can't* hear you. That's how deep I am in the zone.

No, I have no idea that it's been four hours since I closed the door and began furiously typing. Really, the only things I know are (a) when my coffee cup is empty, and (b) when I need to head to the bathroom.

Yes. When you successfully penetrate the zone, there is a chance I'll be an asshole. In fact, I might snap.

The Snap

This is where I apologize.

No one deserves to be on the receiving end of *the snap*. All you were really doing was coming in to see when I was done because we agreed we'd go surfing this afternoon. Still, I got in the zone and I'm writing this wicked article and *who are you and what do you want?* The snap is a glare, a raised voice . . . something designed to indicate you are *pissing me off* with your presence.

It's not fair, I realize that, but think of it like this: if you walk up to me and slap me across the face, I'm not going to think, "Why'd you do that?" I'm not going to take the time to dissect the situation. My instinct is going to be pure, primal, and immediate. I'm going to slap you back.

The reason for this irrational reaction is antiquated brain wiring. Four million years ago it was to my evolutionary advantage to respond to slaps as quickly as possible because they were often precursors to being eaten. Rather than piping my slap response through the "What is a reasonable response?" portion of my brain, it's wired straight into my "React immediately or else" area. Somehow, the snap response has the same wiring. Invasion of the zone is akin to some primal activity that required the brain to wire itself for immediate, irrational response.

It's not right, it's not socially acceptable, and I regret my actions 30 seconds later, but in 20 years of nerdery, the quest hasn't been to kill the snap, but figure out how to manage it.

The Place

Try as I might, I don't always make it to the zone. I'll go through all my odd little pre-zone activities of drink and music selection. I'll slightly adjust the five essential objects on my desk and I'll begin . . . playing World of Warcraft.

This is not the zone . . . this is *the place*. It is very similar to the zone in appearance, but mentally, it's a different muscle that I'm exercising. If the zone is akin to playing power forward in a championship hockey game, the place is the six hours spent in the weight room the day before. Yes, I'm working out my mental muscles, but I'm not really doing anything.

The rule is this: your significant other can interrupt the place with impunity. I might snap, but if you let me linger in the place like you should let me work in the zone, you'll never see me. If you walk into my office to ask me something and see a half-naked night elf dancing on my screen, you are hereby authorized to invade. Mistakes will happen and you'll invade the zone thinking that it's the place, but after I've cooled down, it's my responsibility to explain why what looks like the place is actually the zone.

Other Places

Nerds are rewarded for structure. We get big bucks for reliably generating useful technology that works. Sure, we're artists, but it's an art of patterns, repetition, structure, and efficiency (I swear, it's sexy). This makes it not surprising that the places we create in our homes and in our minds are designed in the same fashion.

The risk with these places is the same risk with all comfortable places. In the comfort, we forget that some of the most interesting stuff happens elsewhere.

Meeting Creatures

Worst meeting ever.

It's not that the attendee list is wrong. All the right people are there and they're bright and they're the decision makers. It's not that the topic is boring or poorly defined. It's a big deal. The problem with this meeting is that it's never going to end.

See, about a year ago, one of our senior engineers was reading our contract with our application server; he read, "Support ends in two years. We're done. You're on your own." He freaked out, called a meeting, and freaked out again in the meeting to make sure it was a big deal, so we agreed it was a big deal. To-do lists were generated, follow-up meetings were scheduled . . . it all had a pleasant "Look what we can do when the sky is falling" vibe. Love it when folks scurry with purpose.

Present day. It's *a year* later and we haven't made the switch. The senior engineer who raised the red flag a year ago is, surprisingly, actually in this version of the meeting, although he is a shell of the engineer he was a year ago. I guarantee he's not going to say a thing because he knows what I know . . .

. . . this is the worst meeting ever.

We knew nine months ago what we needed to do to make the transition to the new server application, but the problem is, it's really fucking scary. It's one of those "We're not going to know half of what we need to do until we start" scenarios, and starting means betting the company. Once we begin the transition, there is no going back and this scares the hell out of everyone, including the VP who will not make a decision.

Each month for the past 12 months, we have had the same meeting. This is the problem, these are the risks, this is what we know, this is what we don't know. All that preliminary crap takes 30 minutes, and since it's been a month since we last heard it, everyone needs to be reminded of all the intricacies. Heads nod while I slowly dig my nails into the conference room table. We then begin the chasing-our-tail portion of the meeting, where all the same questions are asked and answered again. This is why the senior engineer is no longer engaged. He's tired of repeating himself.

Meetings are composed of people, but more interesting, meetings are composed of creatures. These are the roles, traits, and quirks of the people who show up in your meetings, and after you've sat through a couple thousand, you'll see the same creatures keep showing up. Knowing who they are can help you understand your meeting. Knowing what they do can save you time.

The Anchor

Slogan: "It's all about me."

The *anchor* is the big cheese. This is the person that everyone is talking to and this is the person who will decide on whatever needs deciding. When this person talks, everyone in the meeting is listening.

Meetings are power struggles between those who want something and those who don't want to give it to them. If you're walking into a meeting and you need something, your first job is to identify this person. This person is the reason the meeting is happening, and if you don't know who they are, you're missing essential subtext. It's actually pretty easy. Just wait for someone to say something controversial and see who everyone looks at.

There are two major things to be wary of with your anchor. First, make sure they know their job. For standing meetings with the usual suspects, the role is obvious, but for one-time meetings, you can't assume the anchor knows it's all about them. A clear agenda that anoints the anchor right out the gate is the best way to make sure everyone knows who the decision maker is.

Second, you've got to know what to do when there is no anchor present. You're 15 minutes in and you know the senior VP who is actually going to help here is not present. Sure, there are eight other people here that sure like to talk, but the best move is a reschedule. You're wasting time.

Laptop Larry

Slogan: "Pardon me, what?"

Larry is easy to identify. He's got his portable in front of him. That's him right there. If the portable somehow isn't enough, just look for lots of intense nodding from Larry . . . that's him not listening.

Larry pisses me off. He goes to regularly scheduled meetings that he knows are going to be 75 percent irrelevant to him, so he brings his portable so he can work. Turns out he doesn't work because he's spending half his time half-listening to the meeting proceedings. Go read that last sentence again. He's not working and he's not really listening which means he is actually a net negative when it comes to productivity.

Ask Larry to put his portable away. I mean it. If you can't vivaciously participate in a meeting you were invited to, you should not be there. "Rands Rands Rands . . . I take notes on my portable." No, you don't. You take notes and when I use some proper noun you don't recognize, you surf Wikipedia. If notes must be taken, designate one person to do it; I want you asking me what the proper noun is . . . not consulting Wikipedia.

A useful meeting is not a speech; it's a debate. If I'm up there flapping my lips and you disagree or don't understand, I don't want you to nod, I want you to yell at me.

Mr. Irrelevant

Slogan: "I'm just happy to be here."

Why is Mr. Irrelevant here? He doesn't have anything to add, he's just all smiles because someone took the time to include him in what must be a very important meeting. He is mostly harmless.

The problem that needs solving with regard to Mr. Irrelevant is figuring out who invited this guy to the meeting. What were they trying to do? Why is it that you're paying Mr. Irrelevant to sit in this meeting, nod a lot, and take notes? If you uninvited him, he's not going to be pissed, but the question is, who is going to be pissed? Why did they invite Mr. Irrelevant? Is he a mole? Is someone gathering essential information because they can't be there?

There is a reason Mr. Irrelevant is in your meeting and you need to understand that reason before you punt him.

Chatty Patty

Slogan: "I don't shut up."

Another easy identification. This one never shuts up. Ever.

Your main issue here is time. Chatty Patty is incapable of conveying thoughts in a concise manner, which means every time she opens her mouth, everyone else is checking out.

Your first job is to figure out whether Chatty Patty is actually Ms. Irrelevant. Fortunately, getting her talking is no issue. Your job is to figure out whether the signal-to-noise ratio is acceptable. Once you've determined if she actually needs to be there, you next job is containment and, to do that, you've got to play her game.

Containing Patty is a simple process of asking questions in a manner that she wants to hear, meaning with lots and lots of words. Questions for Chatty Patty must be precise so she can't verbally wander. Rather than ask, "How is QA?" you ask, "Patty, I've read your test plan, your current test results, and I understand you have a brief assessment for us regarding the quality of the product. Could you please give us a brief assessment?"

You're going to feel silly constructing these lengthy requests, but not only are you giving Patty a well-defined space to wander in, you're also saving time for everyone in the meeting.

Warning: Don't ever ever argue with Chatty Patty in a meeting setting. Combining Patty's natural loquaciousness with emotion is a recipe for disaster. Remember, she already doesn't know how to end a thought. Throw some emotional in there and she might never stop.

Translator Tim

Slogan: "I know every acronym ever. FTW!"

Tim is the first of two utility creatures. His role is simple: he speaks the language of everyone in the room. When hardware and software get together to talk about the issue, Tim is the guy who translates software acronyms into hardware acronyms. Tim is essential when you've got groups of folks who come from very different parts of the organization.

You need to be wary if Tim isn't neutral with regard to the topic that he's translating. If he's biased, he's translating in his favor, which means if Tim is on your team, you're in a good shape. If he's not, you might want to go find your own Tim.

Sally Synthesizer

Slogan: "What he's saying is . . ."

I love Sally because Sally's job is to end meetings. As our second utility creature, Sally grabs the conversation, no matter how messy it might be, and derives the basic truth of what was just discussed.

In large group meetings with a diverse set of personalities, you must have a Sally in the room because she's not missing a thing that's being said and, more importantly, she's aware of the relative significance not only of what is being said, but also who is saying it. She knows who the anchor is, she knows how to shut Patty up, and while it might appear that she's just stating the obvious, she's providing essential forward momentum to the meeting.

Like Tim, if Sally is biased in a meeting, she's synthesizing in her favor. Also, Sally can get drunk with power because her skill is invaluable. When she starts to think she's an anchor, you've got a problem.

Curveball Kurt

Slogan: "The sky is pancakes."

Kurt is easy to identify. You have no clue what he's talking about.

The first order of business once you've identified Kurt is figuring out if he's Mr. Irrelevant. This can be tricky since whenever you ask him a question, you see his lips move, he's clearly speaking English, but you have no idea what he's trying to say. Hopefully, Translator Tim or Sally Synthesizer is in the room to help out here.

Your absolute worst situation is when your anchor is a Curveball. It happens more than you'd think. The most likely case is combining groups on vastly different parts of the organization chart. Think of executives brainstorming with engineers. Every executive wants to think they can chum it up with anyone in the organization, but when it comes to their day-to-day job, they literally speak a different language. This means you've got Curveball Kurt on both sides of the table. This is an impossible meeting without some type of translator and synthesizer in the room.

The Snake

Slogan: "I'm actually the anchor. Sssssssh!"

Some anchors like to hide. It goes like this:

Big meeting with the executives. Sally gets up, sets the agenda, asks Larry to please, for the last time, put the laptop away, and then the meeting begins. Curveball Kurt gets up and says something unintelligible. Translator Tim jumps is and translates for Kurt, but he translates to the executive in the *right* corner. Aha! There's your anchor. Pay attention to the *right* corner.

The meeting proceeds. Mr. Irrelevant says something funny, everyone laughs and then wonders when someone will remove this boob from the meeting. Finally, we reach the crescendo of the meeting and the decision needs to be made and all heads turn to the anchor. We wait for a second and he says, "Snake? Your thoughts?"

The *snake* is the anchor in hiding and he's in the *left* corner. For some reason, he's got the fake anchor out there taking the heat while he sits there taking it all in. Maybe he doesn't like the spotlight. Maybe there is some strategic advantage to the room not knowing he's the man, but he is. Fortunately for everyone, the snake move only works a few times within a company before word gets out who the real anchor is.

Back to the worst meeting ever. It's the last one I ever attended because when I walked in, I knew what the problem was. We all thought we had an anchor in our VP of engineering, but, the problem is, he wasn't willing to assume the anchor role. Since we had a bet-the-company decision on the table, we should've grabbed the CEO the moment it was clear the VP couldn't anchor the meeting.

You might think we were also missing Sally Synthesizer—someone to capture the essence of what happened—but that was me. I was trying to move the meeting forward by capturing the major thoughts, repeating them for everyone to hear, but it was a useless task since the anchor didn't want his job.

Forty-five minutes after the meeting began, I did something I'd never ever done before. I walked out of a meeting where I was a key player because I simply couldn't waste any more time on this uselessness. Stood up, walked out, and slammed the door. Yes, it's an emotional move that is almost always a bad move in business, but near the top of my list of professional pet peeves is the following:

Do not waste my time.

Incrementalists and Completionists

I recently got into a war of words with a coworker regarding the proper solution to a problem with one of our products. As an aside, let me say that e-mail is never ever ever never ever the right way to resolve controversy. Too much subtlety is lost when you're YELLING IN ALL CAPS at your program manager. Don't waste your time solving problems in e-mail. Stand up. Walk down the hall. And look the person in the eye. You'll live longer.

Anyhow.

What was intriguing about my e-mail exchange with the coworker was that we weren't disagreeing about whether or not we should do something about the problem. We were arguing about how much we should do. The disagreement reminded me that there are two distinct personalities when it comes to devising solutions to problems: *incrementalists* and *completionists.*

Incrementalists are realists. They have a pretty good idea of what is achievable given a problem to solve, a product to ship. They're intimately aware of how many resources are available and the shape of the political landscape with regard to the problem, and they know who knows what. They tend to know all the secrets and they like to be recognized for that fact.

Completionists are dreamers. They have a very good idea how to solve a given problem and that answer is *solve it right*. Their mantra is, "If you're going to spend the time to solve a problem, solve it in a manner so that you aren't going to be solving it *again* in three months." I used to think that architects were the only real completionists in an organization, but I was wrong. Architects are the only recognized completionists, but the personality is hiding all over the place.

Rewind to my situation. The actual problem is irrelevant, but here's the background. The coworker discovered a problem in our product and reported it. I responded and suggested a minor improvement that didn't solve the core problem, but was achievable given our schedule. The coworker responded with, "Why do this if we don't solve the problem?" I responded, "We don't have time to solve it and something is better than nothing." Coworker: "This is less than nothing!" Insert stunned silence.

Remember, the coworker identified (correctly) the original problem. So, why in the world don't they see the value of my solution? The reason is that this is an incrementalist doing battle with a completionist. This isn't a battle of wrong versus right; it's the battle of right versus right. Bizarre.

How does anything get done with incrementalists and completionists arguing about degrees of rightness? Here's the trick. You want them to argue, you just don't want them to kill each other. This is where you, the manager, come in.

Somewhere in the Middle

First, we're going to ignore the problem that has your incrementalist and completionist at each other's throats. It's important, but it's not what we're working on here, which is getting some value out of these unique perspectives.

What's important is, who needs to move where? Does the incrementalist need to move closer to the completionist's view or vice versa? In either case, you've got to use the simplest trick in the conflict resolution book: finding common ground. A better way to think about this is, "What do these disparate philosophies need from each other?"

Incrementalists Need Vision

What defines an incrementalist's day is the raw amount of stuff they do. How many meetings? How many bugs do they close? They love the fact that they ran into that engineering manager in the cafeteria who dropped that critical piece of gossip. Motion, motion, motion.

From the outside, it might look like your incrementalist lacks purpose, but look at the name. This person is driven by the goal of constantly—incrementally—making progress, moving forward.

The question is: What is the purpose behind all this movement? What is their goal? What I've noticed with the incrementalists in my life is that for all the motion, it's not always clear in what direction they are headed. It's hard to figure this out because they look so busy, but the question is, what is the nature of the busy?

Your goal with your incrementalist is to get them to define or see the plan from soup to nuts. This is a big deal for them because they normally can't see past the next meeting. Getting them on board with the big picture gives them a sense of foundation they don't usually have.

This is where your completionist comes in.

Completionists Need Action

Completionists spend much of their lives shaking their heads, staring at the floor, muttering, "Boy, could they fuck this up more?" Fact is, for any given technical or product problem, there's a completionist who knows exactly what to do. Problem is, not only can they see the immediate solution; they see the two-year solution and the five-year solution. By the way, the five-year solution drastically changes the immediate solution, which is why everyone else has a problem with it. Everyone else has no insight into the five-year solution.

Feel dumb? I do.

Now put yourself in the completionist's shoes. Sitting there watching these incrementalists with their rapid-fire buzz-speak, pushing a short-sighted corporate agenda that is clearly going to fail. No wonder folks are yelling in the hallways.

With all of their strategic vision, completionists often lack common corporate and people sense. Yes, they have a five-year technical roadmap in their heads, but they have nary a clue how to start pushing that agenda with the 12 different people who need to get on board to make anything happen. This is why completionists often get incorrectly labeled as curmudgeons. Sure, they're cranky, but it's not cranky for crankiness's sake, it's because they don't have the communication and people skills to convince the company of the truth.

Coffee Addictions

I'm painting a picture of absolutes regarding incrementalists and completionists, but there are dangerous variants that you need to be aware of, and all of these are caffeinated mutations of the core personality.

Incrementalists drink a lot of coffee because of their addiction to motion. Getting lost in this addiction means that incrementalists never finish a thing. They have no concept of "done" because done would mean no more motion and who wants to stop? The warning signs you're looking for here are that when an incrementalist is facing a hard problem, they're constantly coming up with new ways to tackle the problem rather than actually tackling the problem.

Completionists drink a lot of coffee because of their addiction to thought. Unlike incrementalists, these completionists aren't actually saying anything because they're deeply considering the problem. Now, you've got to give completionists time to figure out the plan, but after a significant amount of time, you need to figure out whether they're good at gripping the bat or swinging it.

A quiet completionist doesn't mean they don't have anything to say, they're just unlikely to speak until their plan is fully formed. Your issue is when your completionist has slipped into creative strategic nirvana, where actually finishing something is less important than considering it.

See It Yet?

It's a really simple puzzle. One personality has all the skills necessary to get stuff done, but isn't exactly sure what to do. The other personality knows exactly what to do, but doesn't know how to do it. Your job as a manager is to find and marry these personality types in your organization, because when they understand each other's strengths, you've got a complete strategically tactical product team.

Being incremental and being a manager means I'm looking for one thing out of the completionists on my team. I want to be sitting across the table from them seeing the look of understanding in their eyes, and the look says this: "Hey, I know what you're about. I don't trust it, but I understand that I need what you do, so I'm going to sit here, arms folded, and we're going to fig- ure out how to work together."

Both incrementalists and completionists are defined by a common goal. They both thrive on getting stuff done. This makes them essential to any cor- porate agenda and you want a diverse population of both. Yeah, they're going to argue, but it's the argument you want your teams to have. It's not a fear-based "Should we or shouldn't we," it's "Let's do this thing, let's make sure it gets done, and let's make sure it gets done right."

Organics and Mechanics

Stop. Grab a pencil and write down the first and last names of your past three managers. Stare at those names for a bit and relive those months or years of reporting to this person. I want your off-the-cuff opinion about each one.

My guess is your opinion falls into one of three buckets:

I love this guy. Best manager ever. I still talk to him on a monthly basis because this guy taught me everything I know about what I do. He is my mentor.

Mostly harmless. This guy doesn't really challenge me, but then again, he's not really slowing me down. I'm not learning much, but I don't have to put up with much bullshit. Also, I'm not sure what he actually does, but he leaves me alone . . . so . . . whatever.

Worst. Manager. Ever. This guy makes my life a living hell. I dread our weekly one-on-one. I prepare for an hour and we still end up talking about random useless crap. It's like we're speaking a different language. I don't know what he wants, and even if I did, I wouldn't want to give it to him because I'm so annoyed. I mostly want to give him a poke in the nose.

I want to talk about Worst Manager Ever because, chances are, you're right . . . you are speaking a different language and he's just as frustrated as you.

As an individual contributor or a manager, you interact with two populations: those you work with and those you work for. The conversations with these two populations are distinct. With coworkers, you speak the Truth. You speak it because each of you are slogging out in your respective trenches, so what good is there to say anything but the Truth?

With managers, you speak the Way. The Way includes the things we shall do to achieve organizational enlightenment. "Verily, I shall scribe a specification and it will be a good thing" or "Yea, it came to pass, I say unto you, I am working weekends." The Way is however you're communicating up to your manager. It's different content and it's different tone, and if you believe you have the worst manager ever, then you're not doing it right.

In order to understand how to speak to your manager, you've gotta figure out how they acquire information, and chances are, they gather it either *organically* or *mechanically*.

The Itch Perspective

Your first job is to figure out whether you're working with an organic or a mechanic. To do that, think of any problem as a very complex itch. Now, this is no normal itch, it's a complex itch and scratching said itch is going to take some work. Here's the inner dialog for a mechanic and then an organic regarding how they're going begin their scratching:

> **Mechanic:** "An itch. Well. This itch seems familiar. In fact, I scratched this type of itch in January 2001. Let me first dig up my notes regarding that itching. Excellent. We're going to need a matrix. The vertical column will be action items I can think of that will assess different scratching scenarios and the vertical axis will measure our progress against these different scenarios. OK, we're going to need a meeting to form a committee . . ."

> **Organic:** "Wow, an itch. Hmmmm . . . well, this sucks. Hey Frank, we've got an itch . . . whaddya think? Yeah, that's what I was thinking. You know, this itch seems familiar . . . I think I'm going to deeply consider this itch while I drive home, but first, where's Mary? She knows all about itches and I bet she'll have some ideas . . . I wonder what happens when I type itch in Google . . . *Hey* . . . there's an idea . . ."

Mechanics move forward methodically. They carefully gather information in a structured manner and store that information in a manner that makes it easiest to find again. They quietly observe, they stay on message, they are comfortably predictable, and they annoy the hell out of organics.

Organics are all over the place. They tend to be loud and they can tell a joke. They ask seemingly meaningless questions. They lean forward when they talk to you. When confronted with a horrible situation, you're going to think they're insane because they appear to be still smiling.

A large part of the interpersonal conflict at work can be summed up in the following scenario:

An organic and a mechanic are staring at each other across the desk and are thinking the following:

> **Mechanic:** "This guy is walking chaos."

> **Organic:** "This guy is totally uptight."

They are both right because they both violate each other's sense of propriety. Knowing this solves half the problem. The other half is figuring out how the hell to communicate and that's the hard part.

Prior gig, four years ago. I was hired in by the CEO as a director while they continued to search for a VP of engineering. As an aside, let me stress how bad of a career move it is to *not* know who you are going to be working for when you arrive. The 30-minute interview you have with your future manager is a critical piece of information when you decide whether or not to make a move. Here's why.

The VP of engineering showed up a few months later and he seemed like a bright guy. Good technical background . . . a bit quiet for my taste, but I'm loud so we'll balance out, right? Our first one-on-one showed up, so I grabbed my big, black notebook and plopped down in his office and *wham, holy micromanagement.*

"What's going on with this? How is person X? What about person Y? Have we done XYZ task? No, why? Why again? No really, why?" Question question question data data my lord does this guy think I'm sitting around surfing the Web? OK, deep breath Rands, it's his first week and he's gathering information so I'm going to cut him slack. He'll chill out once he realizes I've got things under control.

Nope.

One month later and the barrage of questions is nonstop. This guy peppers me with random questions and I consistently leave his office feeling like I've been doing nothing with *my 72-hour work week.* It's a cop out to label this guy a micromanager. Great, he's a micromanager. So what? I'm still going to walk out of his office on a weekly basis thinking I'm useless. He's clearly mechanical, but so what?

Remember, mechanical managers gather information in structured way. They do this because they aren't great at relating to people, so they let the left brain take over as a means of content acquisition. This means that if you have a mechanic for a manager, you need to push the information in a structured, well-known, and consistent manner.

So, I wrote a status template for my mechanical manager. It started with products and listed current relevant bits for each of the products on my team. Following that, I listed personnel issues team by team. Contractor status, requisition status, vacations.

Each week, I'd fill this template out 24 hours before my one-on-one. This was my first pass, which loaded my brain with this week's content. I'd remember things we'd talked about the week before and make sure that I'd have the most recent data on those hot issues. An hour before the one-on-one, I'd review again and fine-tune. When the one-on-one arrived, I pulled out my printout and started. I stayed on message and I never deviated from the template. Every week. The same structure chock-full of dates, data, milestones . . . anything concrete and real.

Consistency. Structure. He loved it. I literally jumped up and down after the one-on-one where he didn't ask a single question because I successfully predicted every single possible question he might ask.

My VP was a mechanic and he wanted to feel the structure that encompassed dealing with every problem. Guess what, I'm an organic. My one-on-ones start with a "Hey, how the hell are you?" and then they wander. You're going to walk out of my office thinking we just shot the breeze for a bit, but as we chitchatted, I was carefully gathering content. What was your reaction to question X? What questions did you ask me? Yes, I appear to be collecting trivial crap with my random questions, but I tend to gather more information than mechanics because who the hell knows what I'm going to ask.

That's one situation. There are more and I guarantee yours is unique. My advice:

If You Work for an Organic . . .

You've got to trust that they've got a plan even though it may not be immediately apparent. Don't confuse an extremely open mind with cluelessness. Organics often have a more complete picture about what is going down because they are better networked.

If you're an organic yourself, you're going to love your one-on-ones because you'll regularly work each other into a creative frenzy. Topics will vary wildly and the moment they become dull, they'll vanish. It won't feel like work.

If you're a mechanic, you're going to feel a bit lost with your organic manager because you're OK with lightweight forms of micromanagement. It gives you structure. Most organic managers I've worked with can put on a mechanic hat and provide that structure, but you've got to ask because it's not their natural state.

It's true. Organics miss detail as they hurry from place to place.

If You Work for a Mechanic . . .

Like I said above, a mechanic will not believe you're dealing with something until they feel the structure that encompasses a problem you're solving. You must overload your mechanic with data in order to satiate their structured brain. If your mechanic keeps asking you the *exact same question* and none of your responses appear to be the answer, it's time to counter with, "I really don't know what you are asking."

If you're an organic, you will wrongly assume that mechanics don't trust you, and you're right; they don't. You will build trust by acting like a mechanic with them. It takes practice, but since you're already working for one, you've got a great role model. I'm not suggesting you need to transform yourself into a mechanic (which is impossible), you just need to speak mechanic long enough to soothe your mechanical manager. Once he's figured out you've got chops, you can start going organic on him. He'll deal.

It's true. Mechanics rarely inspire organics.

Look Out For...

Like incrementalists and completionists, the most dangerous organic/mechanic type is the switch-hitter. My personal favorites are mechanical organics. These folks have all the slick tricks of organic information gathering, but they've got the astounding organization skills of the mechanic. They know everything and never forget a bit. I mean it.

Organic mechanics are frightening. They have extreme depth of knowledge, but there is no obvious organic thread that ties it all together. Here's the scary part. There is a thread. There is a purpose. They just aren't letting you see it. Organic mechanics will keep you on your heels and just when you think you've figured them out, they'll change everything. I hate that. I mean I love that.

The Answer Is in the Middle

Organics doing battle with mechanics, or vice versa, is a waste of time. Organizational warfare does one thing. It focuses everyone on their peculiar personality quirks rather on than the business and that means you're wasting cash money. Whether it's my manager or my coworker, when I find myself in an organic/mechanic conflict, I think this:

"A purely mechanical organization lacks inspiration. A purely organic organization is total chaos."

Organics fill mechanical blind spots with their intuition and their passion while mechanics create a healthy, solid home where nutty organics can run into things at speed. It's a team thing.

Inwards, Outwards, and Holistics

There are all sorts of intimidating titles surrounding the management caste. Engineering manager, senior engineering manager, director of engineering, vice president of engineering, chief technology officer. While these names are useful in determining where a individual lies in the organizational chart, the names are merely hints as to what that person actually cares about; and you should care what they care about whether you're a manager or an individual contributor.

Like it or not, your boss has as much effect on your career as you do, and they also effectively sign your paycheck every two weeks, and that means food. Sure, you can leave and go elsewhere, but there's a manager there, too, and he's got his own obscure agenda, as well.

There are three distinct classes of managers, each with their own agenda. The common names for these classes are first line manager, middle manager, and executive or senior manager. Again, these names do a good job of giving you a clue where your manager sits on an organizational chart, but they don't tell you what they actually do and how they are motivated. We need a different set of names for that. We need a set of names that don't confuse us with an implied hierarchy.

The Vision Hierarchy

To understand a manager's agenda, you've got to understand what he wants, and the best way to do that is to figure out what he thinks about all day. What is he paying attention to? Where does he mentally stare all day? It's likely one of three directions.

Inwards: These types of managers are responsible for a small team of folks working on a single product or technology. An inward manager's vision is focused on their team and their product. While they're aware there are other things going on in the organization, they don't tend to be involved cross-functionally unless their team has dependency on an external team.

Inwards are often junior managers, but that isn't always the case. Some very experienced managers have settled into a comfortable groove as inwards because they want to stay near the team and near the code.

Holistics: Traditionally, holistics make up the middle layer of management. Whereas the inward's vision is pointed down at the individual team, the holistic is staring across the organization. They are likely managers of managers; responsible for multiple products and multiple teams.

The holistic's main job is to figure out what the hell is going on *everywhere* in the organization. They're doing this because, as we'll see in a moment, they're actually running your company. This is why they're never in their office; they're running around gathering information. This constant information acquisition gives the impression that they are spread thin and, well, they are. There's a ton of information moving around your average-sized company, and staying tapped into that flood is a full-time job.

Wait, don't these holistics have product to ship? No, they have multiple products, but they've hired rock star inwards to get the products built to specification and on time so they can focus on figuring out what to build next and who they're going to need to build it.

Outwards: These are the senior managers. VPs, CEOs. The biggest misconception regarding outwards is what they care about. You'd think their number one priority would be the care and feeding of the company. Wrong. The well-being of the company is the responsibility of the holistics. The holistics are the ones who are spending all the time sniffing around the hallways, gathering internal competitive intelligence, and building empires out of talented inwards.

The outward's vision is focused on the outside world. They care about the public perception of the company, the company's relationship with its customers, the financial community, the world. That's why they're never at headquarters, they're off telling other people what a great job all those holistics and inwards are doing. I'm not suggesting that outwards don't care about the daily professional shenanigans within the company; they do, but they've also hired a group of rock star holistics to run their company. The rub is this: while it's not their job to run the company on a daily basis, they are accountable for it. Tough gig.

Agenda Confusion

These titles get more confusing when you realize that a manager can have two titles. First, there's the title they give themselves and, second, there's the perception of the rest of the organization. In a healthy organization, these roles are the same, but most organizations just aren't healthy.

An example: You might be working for a manager who fancies himself a holistic when the organization has him pegged as an inward. This means he's out combing the hallway looking for strategic advantage when he should really be paying attention to you, the senior engineer who has indicated, loudly, "There is no way this product is going to ship on time." My first thought is this is both an opportunity and a problem. The problem is that your manager isn't paying attention to his primary job, but the opportunity is that you are.

A variation of this confusion is when a title has been granted, but is not being used. How about when an inward has been forced into a holistic role via a promotion? How are these guys going to screw you? Well, it's not going to be through action, it's going be through inaction. See, as an inward, they don't care about the political intrigue over in building 27, they want to design and ship product, they want to dive into the details. Problem is, the political intrigue over in building 27 will ultimately determine that your product is irrelevant. Now you're out of a job because your manager's manager didn't attend that cross-functional meeting because what he really wanted to do was code. Sorry about that.

Possibly the worst example of this confusion is also one of the biggest reasons for micromanagement. When you're being micromanaged, it means two things: first, it feels like you're doing unnecessary work, and second, you feel the person asking you to do this work is being unreasonable. You're right on both counts. Micromanagement is often a result of a manager jumping from one management class to another. Maybe it's an outward who is getting panicky at the end of a result cycle, so he starts acting like an inward. Problem is, everyone knows he's an outward. He sounds like an outward and talks like one, too. Sure, everyone is happy to get some face time with the CEO, but everyone is also wondering why he isn't doing his job—running the company.

Watch for Growth

The progression from inward to holistic to outward is a strategic one. A junior manager starts out caring about the quality of one product and, if they continue to grow, they end up caring about the health of an entire company. Watching this growth is essential to your own professional growth.

What you need to know about your manager is how much he cares about this growth and, more importantly, whether he sees this as his growth opportunity or the team's. Junior inward managers invariably figure out the responsibility and power held by the holistics and outwards, and when they do, you want to watch them carefully. There is a spectrum here with "advantage for the team" on one side and "advantage for the manager" on the other. Eager young managers who spend all their time looking for advantage for themselves are going to screw the team at some point because of their razor focus on themselves. Are they feeding you the bits of information they find or are they keeping it to themselves? If you're not learning something new in each and every staff meeting, you might have a selfish climber on your hands.

Perhaps your manager doesn't care about growth. Your gut instinct might be that this is a bad situation since working for a manager who isn't interested in growing isn't going to grow his team. Maybe. Maybe your stagnant inward is a seasoned manager who spent time getting beaten up as a holistic or an outward. Maybe they got tired of endless information acquisition or maybe they're just great engineers who love to code. Personally, I think these types of inwards are phenomenal employees and managers because they have a wealth of experience. The question is, are they passing that experience on to you and making sure that you're growing?

My preference is to stock my team with holistic managers and inwards geared to become holistics. While an experienced, steady inward is a reliable manager, I prefer the enthusiasm of employees who are ready for the next thing, especially when the next thing for them is my job.

Free Electrons

Back in my Borland days, we were working hard on Paradox for Windows. I was a QA engineer testing the database creation and modification functionality. Jerry, my counterpart in engineering, was working hard, but getting absolutely nowhere.

We were mid-to-late in a 1.0 product cycle, and most of the engineers were slowly moving from development into bug-fix mode, but not Jerry. He was still implementing . . . over and over again. You are screwed because you've given a critical task to someone who is utterly unable to complete it.

Now, let's first give Jerry a break. He was a fine programmer, but he had two major strikes against him. First, Jerry had never programmed for Windows, so he was learning while he was coding. Second, this was also a 1.0 product. Chapter 13 of this book is titled "1.0," but it's actual title should be, "1.0 spelled one point oh my god I'm never going to see my family again." I'll summarize: 1.0 is incredibly hard, and combined with his Windows inexperience, Jerry was in trouble.

Yet, Jerry had pride. Jerry believed that he could pull it off, but being on the receiving end of his code, I observed a disturbing coding practice, which we'll call "moving crap around on your plate." Jerry's approach to fixing his bugs was to move his code around in interesting ways, much the way you used to shove food around on your plate in a feeble attempt to convince your mom that you actually ate your beets. Nothing substantially changes; it just looks different. Another name for this coding practice might be "coding by hope."

The end result with Jerry's code was that each time he'd fix something we'd discover another fundamental problem with the feature. Yes, small, incremental progress was being made with each bug fix, but Jerry was in a losing situation because his basic architecture was crap. When asked for status, his lists of excuses were astonishingly lengthy and believable. They were the excuses of a person who honestly believed he could pull it off and was willing to put in the hours to do it. But all the hours in the world weren't going to help Jerry because he was in over his head.

If you're the manager in this scenario, you've got to make a major change because you cannot release crap. There are companies that do this and end up making a tidy profit. You are not that person, because once you are rewarded for releasing crap, you begin a blind walk down a path of mediocrity that ends up with you working at Computer Associates on a product no one has heard of and that no one cares about.

It's a two-step fix process. We needed to make a Jerry adjustment and then we needed a miracle. I'll start with the easy one.

We needed Jerry. He's the only one who knows what the hell is going on in that pile of spaghetti and he could fix trivial bugs. The engineering manager sat Jerry down and told him we need to focus on quantity. There were scads of trivial little fixes all over the place that had been ignored, and Jerry could handle those. Yes, his ego was bruised, but in a few weeks, Jerry was cranking because people always work better when they're making forward progress on a task they have a chance of completing.

With Jerry on task, we had to face another fact: we were six months from shipping and we had a major portion of functionality that was cobbled together and barely working. In this scenario, you need a unique talent. You need a *free electron*.

The free electron is the single most productive engineer that you're ever going to meet. I have not even provided a definition and I'm guessing a person that fits the bill has already popped into your mind.

A free electron can do anything when it comes to code. They can write a complete application from scratch, learn a language in a weekend, and, most importantly, they can dive into a tremendous pile of spaghetti code, make sense of it, and actually get it working. You can build an entire business around a free electron. They're that good.

There are two classes of free electrons, *senior electrons* and *junior electrons*. Both have similar productivity yields, but the senior versions have become politically and socially aware. In technology-savvy organizations, many CTOs fall into this category. Think Bill Joy. There's always a risk that senior electrons can spin into a technology high-earth orbit where their ideas simply sound insane, but, whenever they talk, you should listen.

The junior versions have all the ability, they just don't have the experience of dealing with people because they spent a lot of their youths writing their own operating system as a fun intellectual exercise. These junior electrons represent the single best hire you can make as a hiring manager. If you get two in 20 years, you're doing something right.

Care and Feeding

If you are lucky enough to have a free electron in your organization, you need to be aware you are dealing with a strange breed of engineer and the care of and feeding of this engineer might be different than the rest of the team.

Keep them engaged. First, there are two primary tasks in an engineering organization: research and development. While the free electron is eminently capable of doing development, their value in the organization is research. They define the bleeding edge. If you leave a free electron in the development role too long, they will vanish simply because they're bored. All engineers like to be on the bleeding edge, but free electrons simply must be defining it. A departing free electron will permanently damage the productivity of your group.

Misdirected free electron intensity can yield odd results. On one project, I assigned a couple of slippery memory corruption bugs to a free electron who nodded quietly and promptly vanished for a week. When he returned, the bugs were fixed and the entire database layer had been rewritten. A piece of code that'd taken two engineers roughly six months to design had been totally redone in seven days. Sounds like a great idea until you realize we were working on a small update and did not have the resources or time to test a brand spankin' new database layer. Oops.

Free electrons sometimes will not engage and they won't explain why. Free electrons are high-functioning and have strong opinions about everything . . . but they may never tell you those opinions. If you're asking them to do something that they don't believe in, they aren't going to do it. Ask all you want. The worst case is when you ask a free electron to pull off a diving save and they nod . . . and promptly return to whatever they were doing before you distracted them with your useless request. One week later, you're going to be expecting the miracle, but the free electron is going to say, "Haven't got to that."

One week more, your hair is going to be mostly pulled out, and then you're going to realize you didn't need a miracle in the first place and that inaction was the right move. Your free electron knew that two weeks ago. They just didn't want to take the two hours to draw the picture for you. Annoying, huh? You'll get over it.

It's a team. All of this advice is directed at your free electron, but you need to remember even though they're incredibly productive, they're part of the team. My advice shouldn't be interpreted as giving free electrons special treatment any more than you give each person on your team your focused attention. There's no need to call attention to the fact that you've got a free electron on your team. Trust me, everyone already knows it.

Back to Jerry

Enter Bernard, Borland's resident free electron. Up until he started poking around the code, I had no idea what Bernard actually did. He had an office. It was full of books. He talked a lot and produced little visible work. "Blowhard" is what I thought.

Bernard started tinkering with Jerry's code on a Friday afternoon. The next Monday, I was able to run through my functional test matrix for the first time ever. By the end of that week, Bernard had closed a majority of the high-severity bugs and was beginning to tread in fix areas reserved for Jerry. The following week I was racing to file bugs to keep Bernard engaged.

That is a free electron at work.

Rules for the Reorg

You've been here.

It's after 10 p.m. and you get a random e-mail from your boss saying, "We need to talk." No additional data except for a meeting proposal that shows up 30 seconds later entitled "Re: Needing to Talk." You sit staring at the screen, wondering what could be up. No rumors of layoffs are in the air; the company is doing fine. You can't think of anything you've done, said, or written that merits a managerial follow-up, so what's the deal?

By the time the meeting shows up the next day, you've been stewing for a good 12 hours, which means you've reflected on every single thing you've done for the past six months so you can be prepared for whatever curveball your boss is going to throw. When you walk in his office, he's already facing you and he's got the org chart sitting directly in front of him.

So now you know. You're about to endure a reorganization.

Your boss is pretty good about it. He comes right out and tells you that one of your groups is going to be moved elsewhere. He explains the justification and asks you for your thoughts. You chitchat a bit more, then he totally blows it: "I held off from telling you because things are changing so much and I didn't want to jerk you around. It's all settled down now."

Hah. Right.

Before I explain how your boss just lied to you, let's first understand exactly what a reorganization ("reorg") is, and then I've got some advice for how to weather the chaos. First, a reorg is not a layoff. Layoffs can occur as part of a reorg, but they are a side effect, not a cause. Reorgs are when teams and products are shifted around in order to account for a shift in company strategy. What kind of shift? Who knows. Maybe the market for your product has changed or maybe the economy is crap. The point is, someone, some-where in the executive chain decided "We need to make an adjustment to the organization structure," and that means a good solid month of chaos.

Below are some useful rules to pay attention to during the reorg chaos, as well as some tips and tricks for surviving it.

Rule #1: Figure Out Your Role

When you first get wind of the reorg, you have a choice. How are you going to participate? Are you going to sit back and watch the fun or are you going to actively dive into the chaos?

You'll likely need to assess the magnitude of the reorg before you choose. You're especially interested in whatever machinations are in play for your part of the building, but the key to remember is that reorgs represent opportunity. Even if this particular reorg doesn't involve your team, it doesn't mean that you can't pitch your boss on fixing a long-standing organization problem in your group.

The opportunity lies in the fact that a reorg makes an organization very limber. Managers across the organization are thinking the same thing as you: "Well, if we're going to solve problem A right now, we should take a stab at problem B since we're going to be mucking with everything anyway." If you've got an agenda, if you've got a change in mind, it's time to consider pushing it because the chances that you can effect change are vastly higher in the midst of a reorg.

If you're content sitting back and watching everyone else pull the strings, there are still some other things to pay attention to.

Rule #2: People Are Paranoid

There is a painfully long period between when a majority of the organization knows about a reorg and when the actual reorg occurs. It's a painful time because it causes employees to start asking basic questions regarding the company. Who is going where and why? Are there layoffs? Why is this happening and do I have a job when it's all over?

The day before the team learned about the reorg, none of these questions were being asked. The team was working in a state of pleasant ignorance where their biggest worry was the next deadline. Now, they're worrying about what the organization is going to look like tomorrow and the simple fact is, no one knows.

Let's go back to what your boss told you: "I held off from telling you because things are changing so much and I didn't want to jerk you around. It's all settled down now."

Read that again. "Things are changing so much" and "It's all settled down now." He's contradicted himself and you hear this when he says it. Yes, he's trying to communicate, but all he's doing is making you paranoid. You're going to walk out of that meeting thinking, "He doesn't actually know what's going to happen," and you're right. He doesn't.

The fact that no one actually knows what is going to happen tomorrow creates a culture of paranoia and that means you need to start listening carefully.

Rule #3: The Grapevine Gone Mad

A major contributor to the rumor chaos around reorgs is the grapevine. Simply put, information that starts out as fact will slowly become more and more rumor as it moves from person to person. Let's watch . . .

VP of engineering to her staff: "They're building a new hardware group under Ted. It's not clear where they'll be getting all the headcount, but one option would be to sacrifice headcount from other groups."

What'd she say? Pretty clear statement of fact. She's trying to give her staff a heads up. Let's keep moving.

Manager of engineering to his staff: "Ted has a new group. We're liable to lose headcount in our group."

OK, what'd he say? He starts with the facts and then follows up with an opinion—he's losing heads. Why is he saying this? Maybe he's been at the company for years and knows how these things play out or maybe he's just guessing. Who knows? The grapevine is officially in effect. Watch . . .

Senior engineer to his friend: "We're losing heads in our group and they're going to Ted's group. Gosh, I hate Ted."

Welcome to a fully developed rumor ready for consumption by the grapevine.

This is a simple example, but it illustrates basic human nature. We want to know what's going on, and when we don't, we're likely to make stuff up using whatever facts are available to give the impression that we do. When you add opinions and biases to this information-creation process, you end up with a steady flow of compelling fiction crossing your desk.

Outside of the reorg, I put a lot of faith in the grapevine because I find there is less mutation of information as it jumps from person to person, but when jobs are on the line, the grapevine goes insane and some radical crap is going to find its way to you. I advise a patient, journalistic policy, where you confirm tidbits of information with independent sources before you believe anything.

Rule #4: Reorgs Take Forever

The time from when you hear about a reorg to when it's actually done is going to be four times as long as you think. Reorgs take forever. Plans are designed, confirmed with stakeholders, adjusted with feedback, balanced with budgets, run up the flagpole with the big boss, and then taken back to the drawing board. While this official process is going down, there are hallway shenanigans going on, as well as individual political players jockeying for headcount by tweaking the grapevine for their own nefarious purposes. All of this results in more information being inserted into the official process, forcing even more iteration.

My advice here is based on the role that you chose. Clearly, if you've got skin in the game and have an agenda to push, you need to stay engaged for the duration. Don't trust when your boss tells you, "We're done," because that means he thinks he's done. He doesn't know about Phil over in platform engineering who still has a couple of moves in him.

If you've chosen the observation role, I recommend sitting back in your chair and enjoying the scurrying. Take comfort in the fact that you're still employed, and hey, if the reorg affects you, maybe a change of scenery is going to do you some good. Don't forget to ask for a window in your new office.

A reorg isn't over until someone important has printed out a new organizational chart and presented it in front of the entire company.

Rule #5: Most Folks Love Reorgs (But Hate to Admit It)

Reorganizations represent opportunity to those who are unhappy with the state of the current organization. As mentioned above, the moment stakeholders hear that there is a reorg brewing, they start working the grapevine to steer the course of the reorg in their favor. When you combine this fact with people's love of gossip, you're guaranteed a big, juicy, drawn-out reorganization.

If you're an observer, you might be annoyed by all the hallway conversation and closed-door meetings, but the fact is, most folks love this shit. Who is getting moved? Really? Wow. No way. He's an idiot! That blows! For some reason, conversations about reorgs sound a lot like conversations about infidelity. People are incapable of shutting up.

The group responsible for generating the most noise around reorgs, ironically, is the group who has the least effect on their eventual outcomes. These are the folks who are lingering in the dark while the management team wades through strategy, political agenda, and fiscal responsibility looking for a plan that gets the company out of wondering who works for whom and starts worrying about building product again.

The Only Rule: Patience

Think of the last contentious decision your team had to make. I'm talking about a big decision where team members were on opposite sides of the fence and you had to spend a good portion of a week sifting through the facts and opinions in order to construct a compromise decision that everyone agreed to, but didn't like.

Now, let's include the entire company in that decision. It doesn't matter what that decision is, what matters is that large groups of people move incredibly slowly. Call it bureaucracy, call it group think, but understand that very large groups of people working together barely looks like working because they move so slowly.

Reorgs affect the entire company. Everyone has an opinion and that means group think of a magnitude you're unfamiliar with. I know you're worried about your job, your team, and your career, but take a breath—I'm sure there's other work to do.

Offshore Risk Factor

Two bad omens in one day. First, the *San Jose Mercury News* reported that US students are forgoing educations in computer science because of worries about jobs being shipped offshore. The second omen was a *real live* college student sitting in my living room echoing the *Mercury News*, "Yeah, I'd like to study computers, but I hear all the jobs are headed to India . . ."

Hmmmm.

The topic of offshoring has been in my head for over five years. During the tailspin years of my startup, our VP of engineering decided to research moving our QA group offshore to save some money. I was responsible for doing the legwork into possible partnerships, eventually settling on three different groups as potential vendors.

Failed. Failed miserably. Didn't even get to the point of discussing real dollars because we quickly realized there was no way in the world our engineering organization could support a remote organization. We weren't a bunch of idiots and neither were they. We were a startup and most startups work frantically on doing one thing: shipping product. And you can't ship product overseas. You can only ship process.

Process. Management buzzword. Curse to the creative. Yeah, I've been to those *Office Space*–esque meetings, too. Some boob with charts and graphs jumping up and down telling your management team about "process improvement." Jesus, is this over, yet? I've got real work to do.

Problem is, Wall Street loves process. They absolutely adore the likes of IBM, a stock valued highly not because of the product it produces, but the process by which it repeatedly gets those quality products out the door. Reproducibility of the success answers the following question for investors: "Are you lucky or are you good?"

Financial types who surf balance sheets think of process as the "intangibles" of business because, at the end of the quarter, when they're counting how much money you made, it's the intangibles, the process surrounding the design, development, and shipping of the product, that made the whole thing possible.

Process is, by definition, dull. Process is a checklist of obvious bite-sized things you must do to get from point A to point B. Process is predictability. It gives groups of people a common framework to get stuff done. Process helps people and product scale. A simple example: the blueprint for your brand new house. How many different people with different opinions stare at that thing all day making hundreds of little interrelated decisions about what to do next? Imagine these folks winging it—just building a house from the heart. I'm thinking it's ten times over budget and five years in development for a house you don't want. If you're lucky.

Big, successful companies have lots of process. There are big fat binders, flowcharts, and an entire language created around the company's product development process. Yes, it breeds out creativity in favor of predictability, but that's why they've got billions in the bank. These companies scale.

These companies know what they need to get a product to market. They know it down to the dollar because, you guessed it, there's a process-analysis process that describes in detailed, colorful PowerPoint where the money is going. This is how offshoring came to be. It was a single pie chart, in the board room, with executives, and someone was yelling, "We're spending 120 million on tech support? Hell, we could spend 10 million if we did it in India!"

The early adopters had some challenges. Time differences. Poor network connectivity. Cultural differences. However, they didn't have a problem carving out their process from East Nowheresville, Pennsylvania, and plopping down somewhere on the other side of the planet. Their corporate processes are a well-defined machine, and whether the resulting product comes from the US of A or Taiwan, the machine still runs smoothly because it's following a rigid specification.

Now you're sweating. You're worried that you're going to walk into work one day and your boss is already going to be sitting in your office, his head hanging low. You've been blindsided. You've been outsourced.

To help prevent this day from coming, I offer you the following process to gauge your *offshore risk factor*. To do this, you need to look at two things: your personal risk factor and your company's risk factor.

Personal Risk Factor

Go ahead and answer the following questions:

- How much process is there in your job? Do you follow a prescribed, rigid work regimen? Do you know what you are going to be doing every single hour of every single day?

- Can you see a flowchart from where you're sitting right now?

- Can you see a work-provided clock (not yours) from where you're sitting right now?

- Do you work in customer service or technical support?

- Are there big black binders that describe the work that you do?

- Is there a glossary for new hires?

- If you work in software development, are you handed specifications from nameless, faceless designers? Do you *not* have a relationship with the people who are responsible for testing your work?

If you answered "yes" to any of the above, you may be at risk. You could be outsourced because your job is so richly defined that it can be documented and explained to any reasonable professional on the planet who might work for much less than you. Sorry. Go capitalism!

Organizational Risk Factor

The other way to assess your offshore risk factor is to look at two things in the organization: the quality of the process and the quality of the product. Use your own judgment here. Do we have process? If so, how much? Does our product suck? Really, how bad?

Lousy process/lousy product: Whether you're at a startup or an established company, you have bigger problems than outsourcing. Your company is about to fail, is resting on its laurels, or is just lucky. In any case, you're not in a sustainable situation, so start looking for a job. You'll be happier elsewhere. Trust me.

Lousy process/good or great product: Most startups who make it through a year or two fall into this category. They've spent millions of dollars getting the product right, but chances are, they've cut some corners on process. This is good news for you because you've got the essential process in your head and that means job security. For now.

Big fat companies fall into this category, as well. This seems odd because you'd think that it'd require good process to build a successful company. Wrong. Great product can cover a lot of process stupidity. The bad news is that the growth potential for your company is limited by the fact that you're probably spending a lot of money on process errors, poor communication, and duplication of effort. The good news is that your company's inability to communicate with itself makes it an unlikely outsourcing candidate. Congratulations. You'll never get rich, but you've got a job, right?

Great process/lousy product: If you're at a startup, again, company viability is your concern. Why all the process? Aren't you worried about time to market? Aren't you worried about selling something that folks want to buy? Who is paying the bills?

If you're at an established company . . . ouch. High risk area. Clearly, your company doesn't have a dedication to excellence, hence the lousy product. More bad news—you're process-heavy and your product sucks, which means the execs are already thinking of way to cut costs because, I'll say it again, the product sucks. This could be the biggest opportunity for outsourcing firms in America. This is sad because rather than fixing the problem of quality of product, the execs are trying to save the company by reducing the run rate rather than fixing the core problem—no one really wants a product that sucks.

Great process/great product: Wow. Where you do you work?

Still Sweating?

Answered "yes" a few too many times above? Well, here's the good news. Now that you know your job may be ripe for outsourcing, you get to do something about it.

Outsourcing exists because of the Internet and its ability to shrink the planet. As I look at my instant messaging buddy list on Sunday morning, I can name ten folks who I've made in the past two years that I consider good solid friends who live nowhere near me. Never met them, probably never will, but we talk all the time. My gut tells me if I had an idea worth running with that I could summon a virtual investigation team together in about a week. If the idea had legs, we could start producing code in a month.

As we grow more and more adept at using this next generation of commu-nication, our ability to work together when we are geographically distant increases. Think of your favorite open source effort. Think those guys are sweating outsourcing? Nope. Job security comes from actively adapting to the world around you.

33

Joe

Actual conversation.

DSL has been off for over 12 hours and that's about my limit. There's only so long I can do without a fresh set of bits, so I break down and do my third least favorite thing to do . . . call customer support.

Customer support frustrates me because of the well-designed ability to do nothing. This is intentional. The support process is designed to filter out the idiots, which means if you want to actually find a living, breathing human being, you must subject yourself to a series of idiot tests. This is why I reserve customer support excursions for dire situations. No DSL for half a day is dire. Let's go.

My first ten minutes on the phone are spent in admiration for how far voice recognition has come. First off, it's working 95 percent of the time, which is significant. I've been making fun of voice recognition for the better part of a decade, so seeing it applied in a real-time business situation is cool. Also, my DSL provider has done something smart with the recordings that guide me along. The recordings use common language . . . sometimes slang. For example:

Voice on phone: If you're looking for information about new DSL service, say "New." If you're having problems with your existing DSL line, say "Problem."

Me: Problem.

Voice on phone: Got it.

Got it? That's slick. This use of relaxed language gives me the impression I'm dealing with less of a corporate monolith, but we're just getting started.

My call proceeds via the automated customer support center and I figure out there's an outage in Sacramento that "could" apply to me. Problem is, Sacramento is 100-plus miles away from Randsville and that's far enough for me to push a little harder, so I do it . . . I say, "Operator."

Here's the transcript:

Real voice on phone: Hi, thank you for calling SBC. My name is [pause] Joe. How many I help you?

Now, I'm always terribly nice to customer support folks. Even though I've just spent 30 minutes jumping through idiot hoops to get to them. They're just doing their job and being kind sometimes helps.

Me: Joe, hi. My DSL has been offline for 12 hours now and I'd like to get some information about when I might get my DSL back.

Joe: Let me first start by apologizing on behalf of SBC for this inconvenience. Can I have your DSL account number, please?

Joe's laying it on a bit thick, but OK. Whatever.

Me: Sure, it's ###-#####.

Joe: Thank you. Sir, if may ask, what is your name?

Me: It's Rands Pantalones.

Joe: Thank you. Sir, if I may ask, may I call you by my first name?

OK, what the hell? Now, you should've guessed this is clearly outsourced customer support. No big news there. It's also pretty clear that "Joe" is reading from a series of carefully scripted cue cards. Even if his delivery wasn't so stilted, the content of the questions just screams *focus group–derived feel-good conversation techniques*. Let's move on.

We continue. He tells me what I already heard from the automated customer service. There's an outage, but it's over 100 miles away and I want to make sure I'm a part of that 100-mile radius, so I push Joe a bit.

Me: Joe, Sacramento is far away. Can you confirm that my outage and the Sacramento outage are the same thing?

Joe: [Long pause.] Rands, let me again apologize on behalf of SBC for this inconvenience. A moment please. [Another long pause.] Rands, do you like sports?

Right, OK, now you've blown it Joe.

I realize the cue card says, "Choose from one of the following *make a connection with the customer* questions," but I'm becoming more comfortable with the thought of dealing with the voice recognition system than Joe. It's not that I believe Joe isn't a decent human being . . . he's just on the other side of the planet and I don't know shit about cricket and he knows less about ice hockey, so why are we doing this dance?

My discomfort with the Joe experience would be good segue into an incensed rant on the evils of outsourcing, but I don't want to go there. I'm happy Joe has a job and I'm sorry about whoever lost their job back in the States, but I have one piece of advice for both of you.

Cogs get outsourced.

Key Exports

Last month, I spent an hour explaining to the dean of a local college what kind of curriculum he should be schlepping to the local Silicon Valley kids. His first question was, "What is your hardest technical question?"

Before I answer, a brief aside. Yes, I've lost some sleep worrying about the perception that high tech jobs are being shipping overseas. More importantly, I've fretted that declining enrollments in computer science programs are a direct result of this outsourcing. A decrease in the programming population in the US of A would mean it'd be harder for me to hire a fresh-out-of-college guy/gal to beat up for a few years, but I've got some really good news for you.

The next generation already knows more about computers than you do and they haven't even made it to college yet.

The current generation never knew a home without a computer. They assume they have ready access to just about any piece of information . . . and they're probably working on their own Linux distribution right now. As a means of shaping your brain for critical thinking, I'm going to give college two thumbs up. As a requirement for doing great work in the software development industry, I'm going to give a college degree a long "hmmmmmmmm" while I slowly stroke my goatee.

Back to the question, "What is Rands's hardest technical question?"

Me: I don't ask technical questions.

Listen, if you're sitting in my office for an interview, I am assuming you've got technical chops. We wouldn't have let you in the door unless we could figure out from looking at your résumé that you had the technical skills to do the job. Doesn't matter if you're a college hire or Mr. Lord of the Database. I'm not vetting you for technical ability, I'm vetting you for the breadth of your vision, I'm measuring your ambition, and I'm looking for a sign that you believe you can change the world. Really. If all you want to be is a cog in the machine, quietly hiding in the 27th floor of the Behemoth Corporation, Inc., well, that's great, but here's the deal: cogs get outsourced.

Jobs that can be "well specified" are being shipped offshore. High tech moved manufacturing offshore a long time ago and now we're in the midst of pushing technical and customer support there. These are jobs that can be described with a flowchart, a specification, a means by which the job can be performed in a reliable and measurable way.

Think about Joe's job. He's spending his day following a well-defined routine. These are the calls and this is the flowchart. Joe has a daily metric. Joe, you are successful if you resolve 27 calls per day. More is good. Less is bad. The definition of this metric is why SBC is OK with outsourcing their customer support overseas. They did the math. 27 calls a day in the US is $50 and 27 calls overseas is $30. Multiply that by 27 million calls they do a year and you're talking serious bank.

Joe is happy he's got a gig and so am I, but just because his country provides a better dollar-per-call ratio doesn't mean he's got a guaranteed gig. Watch, two years from now Fezlakistan will burst onto the outsourcing stage and guess how long it'll take your corporate behemoths to do the math and start shipping their cogs there. Sorry, Joe. Keep reading. I can help.

Interfacing with Humans Pays Big Bucks

Well-defined QA and engineering is right on the tail of manufacturing and that's A-OK with me because nothing that I've done in just under two decades of software development has been well defined.

Seriously. I'm coming up on almost 15 years straight of nonstop development, crunch cycles, and fire drills. I work hard on improving process and quality, but it's hard to write a good spec when the VP of engineering is telling you that if we don't get customer X that feature, well, 150 people lose their job. So, make the call, don't sleep for two days to get the product out, or write a spec that is going to make QA and documentation's job easier?

The process weenies out there are now standing at their desks viciously shaking their finger at the screen as they read this. They are saying, "Rands, you just got lucky. You've just been fortunate enough to land at successful companies where these fly-by-the-seat-of-your-pants design shenanigans can exist because the cash is pouring in elsewhere."

Really? Fifteen years, four companies, and six promotions later . . . you think I'm winging it? No, I just look like I'm winging it because I never stop moving.

Seriously, I do not specialize in hardened software that keeps submarines pointed in the right direction. I work on software where the primary user is you, the person who stares at the bleeding edge and thinks, "What's next?" Predicting this future is a messy business. There is a distinct lack of flowcharts. Practically zero spreadsheets. People argue a lot, but they're arguing because the best way to refine an idea is to throw it in a mosh pit of creative people, wait, and then see what emerges.

Jobs in this crazy design arena, so far, are safe simply because

- You can't outsource creativity.

- You can't outsource thinking.

- You can't outsource passion.

Our Peculiar Accent

The number of people needed to create a viable product is decreasing. We need fewer folks who make widgets and more folks who are staring at the entire widget landscape and wondering, "I wonder what happens when I put widget X near widget Y . . . hmmmmm . . . I think I'll call it Flickr."

I'm not suggesting that it takes any less hard work or collection of bright college brains to get these ideas off the ground, but I do know that within the circles I travel, there is a distinct optimism regarding ideas. Folks believe they can do anything. I love to think this sense of entrepreneurial spirit is an American asset, but that's absurd.

If we have to outsource something, let's work on outsourcing that. Let's show the rest of the planet the excitement Borland felt when it started to go toe-to-toe with Microsoft. Let's demonstrate the enthusiasm a bunch of Midwest college kids felt when they realized this browser thing they wrote was changing the world.

If we have anything to share with the rest of the planet, it's our own peculiar entrepreneurial accent.

Secret Titles

What do you do? Seriously, on your business card there is a title. Say it out loud.

- "Senior Manager of Engineering"
- "Industrial Data Analyst"
- "Human Factors Specialist"

Is that what you actually do? Try this: think about the last four hours of your job and give yourself a title. Mine would be "Senior Meeting Wrangler" or perhaps "Guy Who Listens." Last week it would've been "Whiteboard Operator."

When you graduated from college, when you got your first job in your chosen profession, did you think you'd be doing this? No. Whatever you thought you'd be doing when you looked forward to being an "Associate Software Engineer" is not what you ended up doing.

You'd think this title dissonance issue would be a problem. You'd think that the fact that what you thought you'd be doing has nothing to do with what you do would turn into angst, but it turns out, as long as everyone is clear what your secret title is . . . we're cool.

This is a piece on micromanagement.

In hell, there are two rooms with the Rands name on them. Room number one is a room where you are constantly nauseated. If you want to torture me, if you want to make my life miserable, get me sick to my stomach, I will do anything, including shoving my fingers down my throat, in order to get out of a nauseated state. I would rather you shove bamboo shoots under my fingernails than spend a night in bed about to throw up.

The other room contains a single person. This is the one guy who, in my 15 years of management, attempted to micromanage me. The walls of this room are whiteboards covered with to-do lists and at the top of each list is a poorly drawn picture of me . . . crying.

In my mind, the use of micromanagement techniques has exactly one goal. You want the target of your micromanagement to leave the building screaming. There is no good micromanagement approach because *who in their right mind* would want to spend their day managing the minutiae of *someone else's* job.

For those of you who haven't been micromanaged, here's a short list of questions to figure out where your manager stands on the management spectrum:

- When your boss asks you to do something, what level of detail does he use to describe his request?

- Does your boss ask you questions regarding the task?

- Once you've begun the task, how often does your boss follow up?

- Do you feel the urge to check in with your boss whenever you are faced with a decision?

- What is your boss's reaction when you deviate from his prescribed means of making progress?

Micromanagers are managers who describe their requests in great detail, leaving little room for original thought. They devise endless checkpoints to determine that their plan is being followed. This scares the individuals involved into vetting all decisions with their manager. When deviations from the plan do occur, the micromanager fucking loses it.

Can you imagine working in such a soulless environment? Can you see why this is my personal hell? It's not just the utter lack of respect for coworkers, it's the idea that the manager's vision is infallible. My job as a manager is to move the group forward, but they choose the direction because *they are doing the work*.

I'm calming down now.

The common assessment of why someone is being micromanaged is, "Well, my manager doesn't trust me." That's kinda sorta right, but the phrase is missing a key element. What is it that your manager doesn't trust you to do? He doesn't trust you to do your job because he doesn't actually know what your secret title is. Chances are, he knows your official title, but the fundamental problem with micromanagers is that they don't grok secret titles.

I inherited my micromanager via a reorg. My VP was leaving, and my development team was dispersed across the organization. I was dropped into this core technology group working on integration with an early version of Java. I was working for a first-time director (uh oh) who had 15 direct reports (crap) and the word in the hallway was that his project was shaky (screwed).

Our first one-on-one was scheduled at 9 a.m. on the first day I worked in the new group. He began with, "Rands, before you meet the team, I'd like you to successfully fix 50 bugs in the code base and I'd like to be the code reviewer for each of your fixes. After that, let's see about you and writing specifications."

This was ten years ago, but what do you think my secret title was? Probably "Organic People Manager" or maybe "Osmosis Hallway Guy." Anyone who regularly reads my stuff knows that my approach involves stumbling around the hallway asking people what the hell is going on. Yes, the new director didn't trust me, but, more importantly, he didn't trust me to be what I'm actually good at, which is an "Osmosis Hallway Guy."

A micromanager does not trust. That is correct, but, more importantly, they do not know. They do not have an impression—a profile of the person they are managing, so they ignore the person and focus on the tasks. This creates a terrific negative feedback loop where an employee becomes demoralized because they believe the manager doesn't trust them, so they stop thinking and start waiting for the dim-witted, micromanaged cues from this emotionally inept manager who is waiting for . . . what? Hard work? Inspiration? What exactly did they do to create an environment of inspiration? The only inspired work that's going on is the employee's desperate search for a job where they're going to be treated like a human being.

Yes, this pisses me off. Even hypothetically.

Fortunately for my situation, the company was crumbling around me, so the director had his hands full poorly managing a series of layoffs. I escaped a month later for a startup, swearing that if I ever saw this guy in a bar, I'd give him a drunken earful. I still scan the room each time I walk into a bar around Sunnyvale.

I'm going to try to save this chapter that turned into a rant by giving you three pieces of advice.

First, regarding new hires. Managers with new hires who are straight out of college often try micromanagement as a means of molding them. This is a management sin. Yeah, I know they don't know anything about anything, but there is a massive difference between teaching someone about their job and mandating their direction. If you believe that in the virgin career state they can't ask bright questions, you've forgotten what it means to learn. Think back to college—did you learn more in the lectures or in the lab with the teaching assistant? The lab, you say? Why? Simple, you can test your knowledge by asking questions.

Second, regarding senior VPs. At some point of your career, you're going to run into a VP of engineering who randomly swoops into a development team and starts meddling with things. Get a pencil ready because I'm going to give you a piece of advice that I want you to write down and stick in your wallet.

All engineering managers miss building stuff.

Forget about whatever political intrigue brought this VP to your doorstep. He was a developer at some point, and when he is meddling with your stuff, he is telling you, "I used to code and I miss it." Once you've identified one of these repressed coding types, the solution is easy. Schedule a meeting once a week where you give him a demo. Don't prepare for the demo, just bring whatever bits you've got and head over to the VP's office. Tell him, "This is what we did this week," and this is the important part, "And what you do think?"

Yes, you've lost an hour a week, but these meetings don't usually last more than a month. VPs have a full docket of stuff to do and once they've scratched their programming itch with your product, they'll move on. Besides, you got some face time with the big boss. How can that hurt?

Third, and lastly, learn how to say *no* (see Chapter 12 for more about saying no). Another VP took a stab at micromanaging at a previous gig. It was a less dire situation than the first time because this guy was simply socially awkward. It took us a good two years to have a "How was your weekend?" conversation without odd pauses and stuttering.

In our first few weeks of one-on-one, he tried some of the same moves as my first micromanager. I drove home after one of these meetings in a cold sweat. See, I loved the job, which meant I had to figure out how to manage this guy. The weekend before our next meeting, I developed an early version of my communication template. When the one-on-one started, I didn't give him a chance to say anything. It was 30 minutes of me listing off everything I knew about what was going on with my organization and my products, and I did it in a very Rands-like, people-focused tone.

I was showing this manager my secret title: "Guy who knows the people are the business."

Glossary

Traditionally, a glossary functions to clarify terms in a book. The fact is I haven't used many of the following terms in this book, but you still need to know them.

Whether you're a manager or working for a manager, there are those out there who will use the words to confuse you. They'll throw them out in the middle of the room sans definition as a power play—as an indication that they control the conversation. There are versions of these people who throw these words out and act like they know what they mean to achieve the same effect.

The only defense with these word nerds is knowledge.

1.0   The hardest product that you'll ever develop.

360 Review   Feedback gathered from your peers, which is supposed to be included in your focal review. Spending time providing constructive feedback increases the likelihood that you won't be working with idiots.

Action Items   Things you should write down. Failure to follow up on action items results in a gentle erosion of your credibility.

Administrative Assistant   Your best friend as a manager. Admins are heavily tapped into corporate machinations and are often able to work miracles when it comes to getting stuff done. They're also usually tapped into the grapevine.

Agenda   The things that must occur for any given meeting to be completed. If all participants in said meeting are not aware of the agenda, time will be wasted.

All-Hands   A company-wide meeting, usually run by the CEO. If you're a manager and there are lots of surprises at these meetings, you might be out of touch.

Alpha   A milestone in the development process. *Alpha* used to describe an early testing stage of software. No one really uses this much anymore.

Architect   An engineer who knows what he/she is doing. If an architect says something that appears insane, it's worth firing off a couple follow-up questions, as they are often smarter than you.

At-Will Employment   Legal definition that states that both employer and employee are employed "at will," which means they can fire/quit whenever they please. They don't even have to give a reason.

Automation   QA buzzword to describe testing that can be done programmatically. Automation is always pitched as a time saver . . . but it's usually a time sink.

Background Check   A pre-hire check employers use to determine whether or not you are a serial murderer.

Beta   A milestone in the development process that traditionally follows alpha. This used to mean that a product was generally usable by customers—a select group of customers who were willing to put up with things not working quite right. No one is sure what beta means anymore.

Bellwethers   The core set of people you trust to interview candidates.

Board of Directors   The CEO's boss. They can fire the CEO. They tend to set broad corporate policy and have amazing powers of invisibility.

Bonus   Unexpected cash. If you're not seeing these at least every year or so, you're doing something wrong. Your boss should be able to explain what you need to fix.

Bugs   Coding errors by engineers often found by QA. Bugs are a source of significant tension late in a product cycle.

Build   An internal version of a product that is used for testing.

Candidate   A job applicant who has made it into the building.

Cave, The   The place a nerd goes to get in the zone.

CEO (Chief Executive Officer)   The guy/gal in the big office. This is a tough gig. CEOs are usually busier than you can imagine.

CFO (Chief Financial Officer)   The guy/gal who tells you how many PCs or Macs you can buy.

Checked Out   An employee who has already quit inside their head. Whether or not you want this person to actually resign, you should be aware that someone who is checked out brings down the entire team with their incessant uselessness.

CIO (Chief Information Officer)   The guy/gal who tells you whether you can use a Mac or a PC.

Collaboration   A word used to convince you to work with people you'd rather avoid.

Completionist   An individual who absolutely must do the right thing when it comes to designing products. What they lack in practicality they make up for with their phenomenal ideas.

Contractor   A temporary employee who never seems to leave.

Credibility   The amount others will believe or trust you. This is a topic that fascinates Rands to no end. Credibility is as valuable as information, but it's equally hard to measure.

Cross-Pollination   The act of taking an idea generated by one team and vetting it with another. Engineers are full of pride and don't like to do this, but cross-pollination often yields improvements that the original team will never discover.

Crunch Time   A time when there are no weekends.

CTO (Chief Technical Officer)   The guy/gal who tells you which is better, a Mac or a PC.

Database   A handy place to stick data if you like your data organized and structured.

Director   Middle management. These are usually the last managers that are in touch with what the products actually do.

Dividend   A share of profits paid to shareholders.

Domain   A sphere of influence. ("That's marketing's domain.")

Doomed   An essential, unscheduled product milestone where the product team realizes they are way behind and choose to kick it into high gear. This term originated with C-3PO in the original *Star Wars*.

Double-Click   Used to have something to do with a mouse; now it's a heavily overused management term used as a segue to say "Let's explore that a bit."

Drug Test   A process used by large companies whereby new hires are scared into not drinking or smoking for about 30 days.

E-mail   The means by which you get spam.

EPS (Earning Per Share)   The portion of a company's profit allocated to each outstanding share of stock. This doesn't happen at most Silicon Valley companies, so don't get your hopes up.

Fire   Termination of employment; usually used in extreme circumstances. ("He's stealing from us!") It is not to be used lightly, and never without the heavy involvement of HR.

Flame Mail   An e-mail you should not send until you've had a chance to calm down.

Focal Review   A yearly meeting with your manager where your performance is evaluated. It's often seen as a vehicle for justifying raises/bonuses, which overshadows the opportunity to convey actual constructive career advice.

General Counsel   The most important lawyer in the company.

Grapevine   A content-rich source of false information.

GUI (Graphical User Interface)   An aging term used to describe a user interface that doesn't suck.

Heinous   Bad. Really bad. Horrible, sky-is-falling bad. Grossly wicked. Handy term when classifying bugs late in the product cycle.

HI (Human Interface)   User interface at Apple Computer.

Holistic   A manager who focuses his attention across the company, not just on his team. Traditionally middle management.

Holy Shit   The moment when a piece of technology totally blows your mind and/or changes your life.

HR (Human Resources)   Happy people who help you do very unhappy things.

Incrementalist   An individual who knows that better is the enemy of done. Incrementalists get stuff done at the cost of quality and completeness.

Individual Contributor   HR term that describes a single employee who has no direct reports.

Instant Messaging   The replacement for e-mail.

Interaction Design   The hard part of user interface design. Interaction designers are responsible for how a user is going to interact with an application, ideally with the least amount of frustration. Interaction designers know what the word *workflow* means.

Intern   A temporary hire, usually from college, who smiles too much.

Interview   The day you wear a tie. Interviews are where you, the hopeful candidate, pitch yourself to a group of folks who have 30 minutes to figure out if they want to spend 5 years listening to your dumb jokes.

Inward   A front-line manager focused on a single product or team. Inwards don't care much about what's going on elsewhere in the company.

IT (Information Technology)   The most generic term in the world, which describes the folks responsible for that computer on your desk. You probably work in IT and don't even know it.

Job Description   A brief, written description of the responsibilities required for a job.

Layoff   A horrible process whereby employees are terminated because the company either needs to save cash or is otherwise preoccupied with something else.

Leverage   A word often used in close proximity to *synergy*.

Linux   UNIX with an *L*.

Mac OS 9   Old version of the Macintosh operating system not based on UNIX.

Mac OS X   New version of the Macintosh operating system, which is based on UNIX.

Malcolm Event   A seemingly insignificant event during the product development processes that screws up your release in an unlikely way.

Manager   The person who signs your review.

Mandate   Order handed down from senior management. Mandates have one of two motivations: they are either used as excuses to dodge explaining rationale (bad) or they are put forth to get people to stop arguing and start moving forward (good).

Market Cap   Simple math. If a company has 1 million shares and those shares are selling for $10, the market cap is $10 million. Often used as a rough means of comparing companies or gauging corporate health. ("Company X market cap is 40 times revenue!")

Marketing   The folks who gloss over what your product actually does. Essential, as most engineers are unable to successfully communicate with actual customers.

Meeting   Traditionally, a group of individuals getting together to solve a common problem. Often, a tremendous waste of time.

Milestone   Poorly defined, heavily over-communicated date within the software development cycle, where the software development team reflects on how screwed they are.

MRD (Marketing Requirements Document)   A mythical document said to contain "customer requirements."

Multitasking   The ability to do many things at once. Multitasking has heavy interaction with NADD.

NADD (Nerd Attention Deficiency Disorder)   A voracious appetite for consuming information at an impossible rate. Rands gets a quarter every time someone says this.

NIH (Not Invented Here)   Term to describe behavior in which an engineering team will not consider working with anyone's code except their own. It's not that the external code is good or bad, it's just foreign, which means it must be reviewed, reformatted . . . Oh, what the hell. *Let's rewrite the whole damned thing.* Billions of dollars have been lost to NIH. I mean it. Billions.

Offshoring (Outsourcing)   Your job being shipped overseas. This is supposed to be "good for our nation" because being unemployed is a "huge motivator."

Offer Letter   A real document handed to a potential new employee, which describes the terms of their employment. It's important to realize that once a candidate has signed their offer letter, your job as a hiring manager is not done. They are not an employee until their butt is in their seat.

Office   The square box where you live. Some models come with windows.

Office of the CEO   The people who surround the CEO to make sure he/she shows up at meetings on time.

Org Chart   A visual representation of who reports to whom. Org charts are handy in larger organizations for figuring out who you're actually dealing with.

Outward   A manager who focuses his attention outside the company. This person is terribly concerned with how the world views his company. Outwards are traditionally senior management, like CEOs.

P/E (Price/Earnings Ratio)   Determines how much money an investor pays for $1 of a company's earnings. If a company is reporting a profit of $2 per share, and the stock is selling for $20 per share, the P/E is 10—the investor would pay ten times earnings.

Performance Plan   A surprisingly upbeat term that describes a depressing process. Performance plans are written instructions of what an employee needs to do in order to not be fired. Don't even think about doing this without serious HR involvement.

Phone Screen   A brief conversation with a hiring manager or recruiter in which one or two key things are going to determine whether you get an interview.

Process   A seven-letter word that begins with *P*. Process is not all bad news, especially for large companies where immense groups of people waste a lot of time doing the same thing.

Product Manager   Ideally, the owner of a product. This person is clear on what the product is and where it is going. They often have to deal with pesky engineers who believe they know what the customers want.

Program Manager   The owner of the schedule. Program managers are pretty much useless in small companies, but essential in any large product development group.

QA (Quality Assurance)   Individuals who find bugs.

R&D (Research and Development)   Or software engineering or software development. Really all the same thing. Suprisingly little research is going on these days, what with all the incessant development.

Reorg (Reorganization)   Process whereby employees are shuffled about to accommodate new corporate goals.

Recruiter   Person whose job it is to help you source candidates for your req. Recruiters often come off as slimy, but they've got a tough gig balancing good people skills with actually having meaningful conversations with engineers. When you find a good recruiter, stick with them.

Reference Check   Process of calling candidate-supplied references. References are biased, as they are supplied by the candidate, so they are suspect as sources of truth. If you've got any concerns about your new hire, I also recommend digging up back-door references or actually grilling references with real, honest questions.

Release Engineering   Group or individual responsible for building/compiling the product. Release folks live in a confusing limbo where they aren't quite QA, but also aren't quite software engineering.

Req (Requisition)   A virtual document that gives you permission to hire a new employee. Rock on! Acquisition of reqs can be tricky, and once acquired, they are apt to vanish without warning. Use it or lose it. Important fact: From the moment a req is approved, the average number of days to get a butt in a seat is 90 days. Honest.

Resigning   Quitting your job. *Resigning* sounds more professional, but it's the same thing. You can do this whenever you like.

Résumé   A very short document that is intended to describe your entire professional life.

Sales   The folks who sell your product. Not a good source of product requirements, as they are biased by the mighty dollar. Often a good source of discontent, though.

Screwed   A professional inflection point where your chosen course of action will allow you to sink or swim.

Short Timer   An employee who has resigned, but still works for the company. Short timers' productivity decreases as a function of the proximity to their last day.

Silicon Valley   A nebulous area south of San Francisco full of money and very bright people.

Slip   A kinder, gentler word for saying that the product is not on schedule. ("We've got a three-week slip.") Frequent slips are often bad career moves, but slips for the right reasons are a good thing.

Software Development Lifecycle   The time between when someone has a clever idea and when that idea is beaten to death and is no longer making money.

Spec (Specification)   A document that tells you how it is. The process of writing a specification tends to be more useful than someone reading it.

Spreadsheet   A poor man's database.

Staff Meeting   A weekly meeting with all your direct reports. Failure to run this type of meeting on a regular basis will result in a breakdown in communication and much wasting of time.

Status Reports   The weekly ritual where you justify your existence to managers; often a sign of corporate bloatification.

Stock   A piece of paper that you'll never see that says you own part of a company. Stocks are easy—you own stocks. Stock options are more confusing.

Stock Options   A piece of paper that you'll never see that says you can buy stock at a certain price. Options often confuse folks, so I'll explain. You are granted an option of 100 shares of your company's stock at $100. Congrats. When you sell your option, you will only receive the delta between your option price and the current price. So, if you sell all your hypothetical options at $110, you are only going to receive $10 per share or $1,000 (minus taxes). People are getting tense about options these days.

Synergy   A word often used in close proximity to *leverage*.

Technical Support   The person you yell at on the phone when something goes wrong with your computer. You really should be yelling at the engineer that designed the thing, but they never answer the phone.

Temp   A coworker who likely will not be sitting in that chair tomorrow; typically assigned work that no one wants or has time to do.

Termination   The politically correct way of saying "You're fired."

Total Compensation   The sum of everything you are paid by a company. This includes salary, bonuses, and benefits. Total compensation is the dollar amount you should use when comparing multiple job offers.

UI (User Interface)   The sum total of every decision made regarding how a program looks to a user.

UNIX   An interactive time-sharing operating system invented in 1969 so that some guy could play games.

Version Control   A database that keeps track of multiple versions of any given file. Version control is an essential tool for development in groups of engineers.

VP (Vice President)   Usually a direct report of the CEO.

Weblog (Blog)   A representation of a person on the Internet.

Wiki   A web application that allows anyone to edit content. It seems like a recipe for disaster, but it turns out that people like their content tidy.

Windows   The number one desktop operating system on the planet Earth.

Workflow   The manner in which a person uses an application. Designing an application with a particular user's workflow in mind can improve usability.

Zone, The   A magical place where you hit max productivity. The zone is very hard to achieve and even harder to maintain.

Index

Numbers and Symbols

1.0 (first version of product)
    overview of, 73, 191
    Rands hierarchy, 75–80
48 Laws of Power, The (Greene and
    Elffers), 37, 41
360 review, 191

A

accepting invitations, 128–129
accuracy of artifact, 97
acronyms, asking about, 128
action
    completionists and, 155
    delegation and, 13
action items, 191
action per decision, 12–13
active soaks, 90–91
administrative assistants, 191
agenda confusion and managers, 165
agenda, definition of, 191
agenda detection
    figuring out issue, 25
    identifying players, 23
    identifying pros and cons in, 23–24
    as skill, 21–22
aggressive silence, employing policy of, 36
agreement on artifact, 97
all-hands meetings, 5, 21, 191
alpha, 191
anchor, in meetings, 148
annual reviews
    assertiveness and, 57–58

Fez issue and, 54
gathering information on year of work,
    55
objectives for employee, setting, 58
performance and, 54
Skill vs. Will model, 56–57
Apple Computer, 194
architects, 192
architectural diagrams, drawing, 49
arguing
    incrementalists vs. completionists,
        153–155
    via e-mail, 153
argument, having, 129
artifact management, 96
asking
    about acronyms, 128
    dumb questions, 90
assertiveness, 57–58, 190. *See also* saying no
assessing colleagues, 5
assessing offshore risk factor
    organizational, 179–180
    personal, 178
at-will employment, 192
audience for status reports, 104–105
automation, 192
availability of artifact, 97
Avalanche, 33

B

background checks, 192
bad decisions, handling, 70
bellwethers
    cultural, 132

bellwethers *(continued)*
    description of, 132, 192
    technical, 132
    vision, 133
beta, 192
binders, 97
blind spots, compensating for, 10–11
blog, description of, 198
board of directors, 192
bonus, 192
Borland
    free electrons at, 169
    Kahn and, 75
    layoffs at, 15
    Paradox for Windows and, 167
    resignation from, 61, 65
brainstorm meetings
    content, 86
    ending, 87
    evaluation of, 86–87
    players, 85
    scheduling, 85
bug database, value of, 107
bugs, 192
build, 192
building culture, 80
buzzword-compliance, on résumé, 119

C

candidates. *See also* interviews of
        candidates
    description of, 192
    sourcing, 197
capturing context
    of changes, 100
    on projects, 100–101
care and feeding of free electrons, 168
career advancement, coding and, 49–50
career objective, on résumé, 118
career of author, 8
cave, nerd
    description of, 192
    other places and, 145
    place, the, and, 144
    snap, the, and, 143–144
    traits of, 141–142
    zone, the, and, 143
CEO (Chief Executive Officer)
    connection with, 4–5
    description of, 192
    office of, 196
CFO (Chief Financial Officer), 192

changes, commenting, 100
charts, trusting, 75
Chatty Patty, in meetings, 149
cheap shots, taking when resigning, 63
checked out, 192
Chief Executive Officer (CEO)
    connection with, 4–5
    description of, 192
    office of, 196
Chief Financial Officer (CFO), 192
Chief Information Officer (CIO), 192
Chief Technical Officer (CTO), 193
choosing type of manager to be, 4
CIO (Chief Information Officer), 192
code. *See also* coding
    commenting changes in, 100
    as living forever, 48
    writing, 47
Code Complete (McConnell), 44
coding. *See also* code
    as act of creation, 49
    career advancement and, 49–50
    disturbing practices of, 167
    stop coding advice, 47, 49–51
coffee addictions, 155
collaborative, 40, 192
collaborative management style
    debate and, 28
    delivering mandate and, 29
college degree, uses of, 183
commenting changes, 100
communication. *See also* status reports
    during phone screen, 124
    gossip, rumor, and, 34, 194
    with mechanics and organics, 158–160
    process as defining, 78–79
    reorg and, 173
    with Worst Manager Ever, 157
compensating for blind spots, 10–11
complacency, 53
completionists
    description of, 153, 193
    managing, 156
    as needing action, 155
    variants of, 155
computer science programs, 183
conflict resolution meetings, 22
connection with CEO, 4–5
cons
    meeting needs of, 24
    in meetings, identifying, 23–24
consensus of team
    going against on hiring, 134
    on hiring, 133

content
    for brainstorm and prototype meetings,
        86
    of résumé, 120
context
    of changes, capturing, 100
    on projects, capturing, 100–101
    switching, and NADD, 139
contractors, 193
costs of Malcolm events, 95–96
credibility, 193
Critic, the, 108–109
cross-pollination, 50, 193
crunch time, 193
CTO (Chief Technical Officer), 193
cultural bellwethers, 132
culture
    building, 80
    of thinking, 88
Curveball Kurt, in meetings, 151
customer support
    frustrations with, 181
    outsourced, 182

D

databases, 193
debate of issues and mandate, 28–29
deciding when to employ mandate, 28
decisions
    handling bad, 70
    including team in process of making, 70
    of manager, questioning, 69
    missed, as Malcolm events, 94–95
degree earned, on résumé, 119
del.icio.us, 100
delegation and action, 13
delivering mandate, 29
delivering mandate (again), 29–30
designing résumé, 119–120
developing, continuing, 51
development environment, using, 49
Dickerson, Rob, 15
directors, 193
dividends, 193
documenting production, 55–56
domain, 193
doomed, 193
dot-com implosion, 3
double-click, 193
downsides of NADD, 140
drink invitations, accepting, 129
drug tests, 193

E

e-mail
    arguing via, 153
    description of, 193
    flame-o-grams, 92, 193
    forwarding, 36
e-mailing status reports to senior
        management, 106
earnings per share (EPS), 193
Elffers, Joost, *The 48 Laws of Power*, 37, 41
employees. *See also* candidates; teams
    disconnect between managers and, 7
    objectives for, setting, 58
    pruning of, 53
ending brainstorm and prototype meetings,
        87
engineering managers, 189
entrepreneurial accent, 184
entropy always wins, 111
EPS (earnings per share), 193
evaluating brainstorm and prototype
        meetings, 86–87
evaluating manager
    action per decision, 12–13
    compensation for blind spots, 10–11
    language spoken to, 11
    one-on-one meetings, 12
    overview of, 16
    pedigree, 9–10
    as political navigator, 13
    pride and panic, 14–15
evil managers, 8
experience, seemingly irrelevant, including
        on résumé, 120

F

failure
    of pitches, 80
    of startups, 73
Favorite Application, 99
feature, owning, 50
Fez issue, dealing with, 53–54, 59
fighting stagnation, 88
figuring out role in reorg, 172
finding inner circle, 130
finishing job interview, 127–128, 130
fire, 193
first version of product (1.0)
    overview of, 73, 191
    Rands hierarchy, 75–80
flame mail, 92, 193

Find it faster at http://superindex.apress.com/

flexibility, 47, 51
Flickr, 100
focal reviews, 194
foreign mandate, 30–31
48 Laws of Power, The (Greene and
  Elffers), 37, 41
forwarding e-mails, 36
freakouts
  getting to solution, 19
  giving benefit of doubt, 18
  hammering with questions, 19
  intensity of, 18
  as management failure, 20
  on Monday, 17–18
  participating in, 18
free electrons
  at Borland, 169
  care and feeding of, 168
  at startup, 77
future, investing in, 77

G

general counsel, 194
giving notice when resigning, 64
Google, 88
gossip/grapevine
  description of, 194
  as evidence of failure to communicate,
    34
  reorg and, 173
graphical user interface (GUI), 194
graphs, trusting, 75
great manager, definition of, 4
Greene, Robert, *The 48 Laws of Power*, 37,
  41
growth in managers, 165–166
GUI (graphical user interface), 194
guilt when resigning, 62
Guns of the South (Turtledove), 137

H

healthy business, definition of, 53
heinous, 194
HI (human interface), 194
hiring, as huge risk, 135
holistics, 164–166, 194
holy shit moment, 94, 194
Hover, 33
HR (Human Resources), 194
human interface (HI), 194
humility, 38

I

ideas
  need for people with, 184
  writing down, 91
identifying
  issues in meeting, 25
  players in meeting, 23
  pros and cons in meeting, 23–24
impossible tasks
  iteration and, 109–110
  mixing it up, 110–111
  starting, 109
incrementalists
  description of, 153, 194
  managing, 156
  as needing vision, 154
  variants of, 155
individual contributors, 194
influence, exerting and testing, 129
information acquisition, active, 12
information conduit, acting as, 33–34
information starvation, preventing, 35–36
Information Technology (IT), 194
informational meetings, 21
inner circle, finding, 130
instant messaging, 194
interaction design, 194
interfacing with humans, 184
interns, 194
interviews for new job, finishing, 127, 130
interviews of candidates
  bellwethers and, 192
  core team for, 131
  cultural bellwether and, 132
  description of, 194
  going against team consensus on, 134
  success in, 131
  team consensus on, 133
  technical bellwether and, 132
  vision bellwether and, 133
investing in future, 77
inwards
  description of, 164, 194
  growth in, 165–166
issue of meeting, identifying, 25
IT (Information Technology), 194
itch perspective, 158–160
iteration, 109–110

J

job description, 194
job history, on résumé, 119

job of manager, 8–9
job opportunities, scrubbing, 123
job security and offshoring, 180
job titles, 187
Joy, Bill, 168
junior electrons, 168
justifying mandate, 30

K

Kahn, Phillippe, 75

L

language spoken to manager, 11
Laptop Larry, in meetings, 148
layoff
    description of, 195
    handling, 15
layout of nerd cave, 142
leverage, 195
leveraging NADD, 139–140
Linux, 195
listening to people, 4, 18, 36
local mandate, 30
Long Stare, 33
losing it, as manager, 69
losing perspective, 49–50
lunch invitations, accepting, 128

M

Mac OS 9, 195
Mac OS X, 195
Malcolm events
    artifact management and, 96
    avoiding costs of, 95–96
    description of, 93, 195
    missed decisions as, 94–95
    success in avoiding as silent, 97
management, as chess, 37
management skills, as arrows in quiver, 1
managementese, 11, 43–45
managers. *See also* evaluating managers
    agenda confusion and, 165
    classes of, 163
    description of, 195
    growth in, 165–166
    vision hierarchy of, 163
mandates
    credibility and, 28
    Decide phase of, 28

Deliver (Again) phase of, 29–30
Deliver phase of, 29
description of, 27, 195
foreign, 30–31
justifying, 30
market cap, 195
marketing, 195
Marketing Requirements Document
    (MRD), 195
Maslow's Hierarchy of Needs, 74–75
McConnell, Steve, *Code Complete*, 44
mechanical organics, 161
mechanics
    manager as, 158–161
    when working for organic, 160
    working for, 160
meeting creatures
    anchor, 148
    Chatty Patty, 149
    Curveball Kurt, 151
    Laptop Larry, 148
    Mr. Irrelevant, 149
    Sally Synthesizer, 150
    snake, 151–152
    Translator Tim, 150
meetings. *See also* brainstorm meetings;
        meeting creatures
    agenda detection and, 21–22
    all-hands, 5, 21, 191
    conflict resolution, 22
    description of, 195
    figuring out issue of, 25
    identifying players in, 23
    identifying pros and cons in, 23–24
    interview feedback, 133–134
    one-on-ones, 12
    as power struggles, 148
    staff, 35, 198
    wasting time in, 152
metaphors, 44
micromanagement
    description of, 165, 187–188
    new hires and, 189
    secret titles and, 188–190
milestone, 195
mixing it up, 110–111
Monday freakouts, 17
monthly documentation, 55–56
Mr. Irrelevant, in meetings, 149
MRD (Marketing Requirements
        Document), 195
multitasking
    definition of, 195
    NADD and, 139

N

NADD (nerd attention deficiency disorder), 137–140, 195
name calling, 113, 115
navigating politics, 13
nerd cave
    other places and, 145
    place, the, and, 144
    snap, the, and, 143–144
    traits of, 141–142
    zone, the, and, 143
Netscape, next-generation browser project, 13
network, respecting when resigning, 62
new hires, 189
new job
    accepting invitations, 128–129
    asking about acronyms, 128
    completing interview for, 127–128
    finding inner circle, 130
    finishing interview, 130
    having argument, 129
    saying something stupid, 129
    staying late, showing up early, 128
    storytelling and, 127
    telling someone what to do, 129
NIH (Not Invented Here), 195
nothing happens until you start, 109
notice, giving when resigning, 64

O

objectives for employee, setting, 58
obstructionists in meetings, 85
offer letters, 196
office, 196
office of the CEO, 196
offshoring
    description of, 196
    early adopters of, 178
    job security and, 180
    jobs safe from, 184
    key exports, 183
    organizational risk factor, assessing, 179–180
    personal risk factor, assessing, 178
    startups and, 177
one-on-one meetings, 12
opportunity, reorg as, 174
organic mechanics, 161
organics
    manager as, 158–161
    when working for mechanic, 160
    working for, 160

organization (org) chart
    description of, 196
    during startup, 79
organization information, maintaining consistent flow of, 35
other places, and nerd cave, 145
outsourcing. *See* offshoring
outwards, 164, 196
owning feature, 50

P

P/E (price/earnings ratio), 196
panic, handling, 15. *See also* freakouts
Paradox for Windows, 167
Paradox for Windows team, 48
paranoia and reorg, 172
passive soaks, 90–91
patience and reorg, 174
pawns in conflict resolution meetings, 22
pedigree of manager, 9–10
people
    to build Your Great Idea, 76–77
    with ideas, need for, 184
    listening to, 4, 18, 36
    talking with, 45
performance plan, 196
performance reviews, purpose of, 38. *See also* annual reviews
perspective, losing, 49–50
phone screens
    description of, 196
    importance of, 123
    preparation for, 124
    purpose of, 123–124, 126
    questions for interviewer, 125
    reviewing, 126
    techniques of, 124–125
pitch
    failure of, 80
    to stranger, 90
    for Your Great Idea, 76
place, the, and nerd cave, 144
players
    for brainstorm and prototype meetings, 85
    in conflict resolution meetings, 22
    identifying, 23
    pros and cons, identifying, 23–24
point of freakouts, getting to, 18–19
politics, navigating, 13
posting statuses to wiki, 106
power, managers punch drunk on, 68
preparing for phone screens, 124–125

price/earnings ratio (P/E), 196
pride, getting to, 14
process
    as defining communication, 78–79
    definition of, 196
    offshoring and, 178
    stuff-building, 94
    Wall Street and, 177
product
    bug database a source of information on, 107
    career-defining, 90
    in Rands hierarchy, 79
product manager, 196
production, documenting, 55–56
professional objective, on résumé, 118
program manager, 196
pros
    in meetings, identifying, 23–24
    tactics of, 24
prototype meetings
    content, 86
    ending, 87
    evaluation of, 86–87
    players, 85
    scheduling, 85
pyramid of Rands hierarchy, using, 79–80

Q

QA (Quality Assurance), 196
question offense for freakouts, 19
questioning decisions of manager, 69
questions
    asking dumb, 90
    preparing for interviewer, 125

R

R&D (Research and Development), 196
Rands 1.0 hierarchy
    overview of, 75
    people, 76–77
    pitch, 76
    process, 78–79
    product, 79
    pyramid, using, 79–80
reacting compared to thinking, 83–84
recovering it, as manager, 69–70
recruiters, 197
reference checks, 197
release engineering, 197
reorg (reorganization)

dealing with, 171
description of, 197
figuring out role, 172
grapevine and, 173
as opportunity, 174
paranoia and, 172
patience and, 174
time frame for, 173–174
req (requisition), 197
Research and Development (R&D), 196
research and free electrons, 169
resignation checklist
    do right by coworkers, 63
    don't give too much notice, 64
    don't overcommit on deliverables, 62
    don't take cheap shots, 63
    don't volunteer to work after leaving, 64
    respect network, 62
    update Rolodex, 62
    violating, 61
resigning, 197
respecting network when resigning, 62
résumé
    content of, 120
    description of, 197
    designing, 119–120
    first pass, 117–118
    as glimpse and hook, 121
    making impression with, 117
    second pass, 118–119
Rolodex, updating when resigning, 62
rumor, as failure to communicate, 34

S

sales, 197
Sally Synthesizer, in meetings, 150
saying no, 69–70, 190
saying something stupid, 129
school attended, on résumé, 119
screwed, 197
scrubbing job opportunities, 123
senior electrons, 168
short timer's disease, 62, 197
showing up early, staying late, 128
silence, 40
silent majority and mandates, 28
Silicon Valley, 197
Skill vs. Will model, 56–57
slip, 197
snake, in meetings, 151–152
snap, the, and nerd cave, 143–144
soaking
    active soaks, 90–91

soaking *(continued)*
allowing time for, 92
overview of, 89–90
passive soaks, 91
software development lifecycle, 197
solution to freakouts, getting to, 19
sourcing candidates, 197
speaking Truth and Way, 157
specs (specifications)
description of, 198
writing and maintaining, 96
Spiderman, theme of, 67
spreadsheets, 198
staff meetings, 35, 198
stagnation
fighting, 88
warning signs of during 1.0, 79
starting impossible task, 109
startup burnout, 79
startups
crossroads example of, 80
failure of, 73
free electrons at, 77
offshoring and, 177
organization chart during, 79
organizational inflection points and, 103
Rands hierarchy and, 76
status reports
audience for, 104–105
description of, 101, 198
need for, 104
open issue on, 105
three-tiered fix for, 105–106
staying late, showing up early, 128
stock, 198
stock options, 198
stop coding advice, 47, 49–51
stopping impossible task, 110
stranger, pitching to, 90
strategic hires, 133
stuff-building process, 94
subterfuge, 38–39
subtlety, 37–38
success, as silent, 97
surfing entropy, 111
synergy, 198

defining time to start thinking, 85
free electrons and, 169
going against consensus of, on hiring, 134
including in decision-making process, 70
for interviews, 131
meetings with, for thinking, 85–87
members of, as having stories to tell, 127
technical bellwethers, 132
vision bellwethers, 133
wiki for, 105–106
technical bellwethers, 132
technical support, 198
telling someone what to do, 129
temps, 198
termination, 198
test scripts, writing, 50
thinking
creating culture of, 88
meetings for, 85–87
reacting compared to, 83–84
soaking and, 89–92
time for team to start, 85
three-tiered fix for status reports, 105–106
time
for reorg, 173–174
for soaking, 92
titles, job, 187
to-do lists
Critic and, 108–109
iteration, 109–110
mixing it up, 110–111
relying on brain for, 35
starting impossible task, 109
top hat story, 67–68, 70
total compensation, 198
Translator Tim, in meetings, 150
Trickle theory
entropy always wins, 111
example of, 108
iteration, 109–110
mix it up, 110–111
nothing happens until you start, 109
trusting charts 'n' graphs, 75
Truth, speaking, 157
Turtledove, Harry, *Guns of the South*, 137

T

tactical hires, 133
talking with people, 45
teams
consensus of, on hiring, 133
cultural bellwethers, 132

U

UI (user interface), 198
UNIX, 198
updating Rolodex when resigning, 62

V

version control system, 99–101, 198
Vice President (VP), 198
view from nerd cave, 142
vision, incrementalists and, 154
vision bellwethers, 133
vision hierarchy of managers, 163
visual design of résumé, 120
voice recognition, 181
volunteering to work after leaving job, 64
VP (Vice President), 198

W

Wall Street and process, 177
Way, speaking, 157
Web
    NADD and, 140
    writing for, 3

weblog
    description of, 198
    for posting statuses, 106
wiki for group
    description of, 198
    posting statuses to, 106
    setting up, 105
Windows, 199
workflow, 199
Worst Manager Ever, 157
writing
    down ideas, 91
    specifications, 96
    test script, 50
    for Web, 3

Z

zone, the, 143, 192, 199